DRUG DANGERS

The Dangers of
Painkillers

Peggy J. Parks

ReferencePoint
Press®

San Diego, CA

About the Author

Peggy J. Parks holds a bachelor of science degree from Aquinas College in Grand Rapids, Michigan, where she graduated magna cum laude. An author who has written dozens of educational books on a wide variety of topics for children and young adults, Parks lives in Muskegon, Michigan, a town that she says inspires her writing because of its location on the shores of Lake Michigan.

© 2017 ReferencePoint Press, Inc.
Printed in the United States

For more information, contact:
ReferencePoint Press, Inc.
PO Box 27779
San Diego, CA 92198
www.ReferencePointPress.com

LIBRARY OF CONGRESS CATALOGING-IN-PUBLICATION DATA

Names: Parks, Peggy J., 1951– author.
Title: The dangers of painkillers / by Peggy J. Parks.
Description: San Diego, CA : ReferencePoint Press, Inc., 2017. | Series: Drug dangers series | Audience: Grade 9 to 12. | Includes bibliographical references and index.
Identifiers: LCCN 2015042816 | ISBN 9781682820247 (hardback)
Subjects: LCSH: Analgesics--Juvenile literature.
Classification: LCC RM319 .P38 2017 | DDC 615.7/83--dc23

LC record available at http://lccn.loc.gov/2015042816

CONTENTS

When Jeremy Brooking was growing up in southern Indiana, he often dreamed about joining the US Marines. "Ever since I was little, I knew that's what I wanted to do,"[1] he says. As the years went by, he remained certain that he would join the marines as soon as he was old enough. In late 2006, about six months after graduating from high school, Brooking went to a recruiting office and enlisted. It seemed like a dream come true—but then the dream was shattered by a life-threatening injury and subsequent addiction to painkillers.

No Way to Live

Brooking was deployed to Iraq in April 2007. The following month, while on patrol in the town of Fallujah, his outpost came under heavy fire, and he was shot by an Iraqi sniper. The round pierced his bulletproof vest and tore through his chest, lodging just above his heart. His condition was grave; on the way to the hospital he coded twice and was revived. In a telephone call to Brooking's wife, his fellow marines said that he was severely wounded, had lost a lot of blood, and probably would not survive. Yet despite the overwhelming odds against him, he made it through surgery and after a period of recovery was sent back home to Indiana. That, says Brooking, was the start of his living nightmare. "Getting shot was just the beginning. After I got home, that's when the real battle began."[2]

Because of the severity of his injury, Brooking suffered from excruciating chest pain, for which his US Department of Veterans Affairs (VA) doctors prescribed painkillers—massive amounts of them. At one point he was taking twenty-three types of pain medication, "easily over 100 different pills a day," he says, noting that a one-month supply of his pills filled a plastic grocery bag. Being so dependent on drugs was ruining Brooking's life and his marriage; he slept twenty-three of twenty-four hours each day. "I'd wake up, eat, sleep and take more pills,"[3] he says. Finally, Brooking sought medical care from a private physician not affiliated with the VA. The doctor took Brooking off all medications except one, Suboxone, which relieved his pain and helped wean him from narcotic painkillers.

When Pain Is Constant

Brooking's situation may sound extreme, but chronic (long-lasting) pain is pervasive among military veterans. According to VA officials, more than half of veterans who have returned from war zones in Afghanistan and Iraq suffer from chronic pain. "It is a huge problem for so many veterans," says US Army captain Darisse Smith. "It's not just traumatic battle injuries—it's also the wear and tear of doing a tough job in a tough environment."[4]

Chronic pain is also widespread among the general population in the United States. It affects an estimated 100 million Americans, according to the National Institutes of Health. That is nearly one-third of the US population—more than the number of Americans with diabetes, cancer, and heart disease combined. Chronic pain is also a worldwide problem. In a July 2015 paper, pain management experts Robert N. Jamison and Jianren Mao refer to chronic pain as "an international health issue of immense importance that is influenced by both physical and psychological factors." Having to suffer from pain on a day-to-day basis can be both depressing and debilitating, as Jamison and Mao explain: "Chronic pain can interfere with sleep, employment, social life, daily activities, and overall quality of life."[5]

There are myriad causes of chronic pain, from severe sprains and strains to aches that linger long after broken bones heal. Those who have cancer often suffer from severe pain because of the disease itself, as well as the treatments associated with it. A debilitating condition known as fibromyalgia is characterized by widespread musculoskeletal pain. Another is peripheral

According to the National Institutes of Health, nearly a third of Americans live with chronic pain. This debilitating condition can take both a physical and mental toll on sufferers. It can interfere with daily activities such as sleep and work, making simple movements painful and difficult.

neuropathy, in which the tips of the nerves going to the fingers, hands, and toes are damaged, causing excruciating pain. "I've been told that it feels like walking on razor blades,"[6] says Charles Kim, a physician at NYU Langone Medical Center. The most common type of chronic pain, according to the American Academy of Pain Medicine, is low back pain, followed by severe headache (including migraine), neck pain, and pain in the facial area, often in the jaw in front of the ear.

Pain Relief

The staggering number of individuals plagued by chronic pain has led to a soaring demand for analgesics, which are more commonly known as pain medications or painkillers. These drugs are available in a wide array of types, strengths, and delivery methods. For instance, painkillers may be taken by mouth in pill or liquid form; as a liquid administered intravenously (typically by a medical professional for the most severe cases); or in topical form, such as ointments, creams, or patches applied to the skin. Analgesics can be loosely divided into three main categories: acetaminophen, nonsteroidal anti-inflammatory drugs (NSAIDs), and opioids, which are also called narcotic pain relievers.

Acetaminophen is an over-the-counter pain medication, which means it is available without a doctor's prescription. A well-known brand of acetaminophen is Tylenol, although the drug is sold under a number of generic brand names as well. This is also true of ibuprofen, an NSAID that is sold as Advil and Motrin, as well as store brands and other generic names. (Stronger versions of Advil and Motrin may also be prescribed by a doctor.) The most common NSAID, aspirin, is also the oldest. Thousands of years ago people used natural sources of salicylic acid, aspirin's main active ingredient, to relieve their pain. "Aspirin is one of those things that, long before there were ever clinical trials or any kind of scientific knowledge, people figured out, 'Hey, I feel better when I take this substance,'"[7] says Karol Watson, a cardiologist with the David Geffen School of Medicine at the University of California–Los Angeles. Today aspirin and other over-the-counter drugs are typically used to relieve headaches, muscle aches, backaches, and other kinds of mild to moderate pain.

For relief of moderate to severe pain, people throughout the world rely on opioids, the strongest of all painkillers. Opioids (often used interchangeably with "opiates") are so named because they are semisynthetic versions of opium, a narcotic that is made from the sap of opium poppies. According to Dr. Francis Collins, director of the National Institutes of Health, as many as 8 million Americans take opioids for chronic pain. Opioids are controlled substances, meaning their possession and use are controlled by law and they are legally available only with a doctor's prescription. Collins says that in 2012 more than 259 million prescriptions were written in the United States for opioid painkillers. "That equals one bottle of pain pills for every U.S. adult,"[8] he says. Surveys have shown that opioid prescription rates vary considerably by state.

A Centuries-Old Epidemic

Health officials refer to America's pervasive reliance on opioid painkillers as an epidemic and public health crisis. Yet even though awareness of the problem is greater than ever before, the problem is not new. "The current opioid addiction crisis is, in many ways, a replay of history," says addiction expert Andrew Kolodny and the coauthors of a 2015 journal article. "America's first epidemic of opioid addiction occurred in the second half of the nineteenth century." This was a time when opioid products were not yet regulated, and use of the drugs soared more than 500 percent. Much like today, the people abusing opioids were from all walks of life. "Mothers dosed themselves and their children with opium tinctures and patent medicines. Soldiers used opium and morphine to treat diarrhea and painful injuries. Drinkers alleviated hangovers with opioids. Chinese immigrants smoked opium, a practice that spread to the white underworld."

In the late 1900s physicians played a major role in the soaring rate of opioid use, but this was largely because they had few options for helping patients who suffered from pain. It was extremely rare for diseases to be cured, since the root causes of many conditions were poorly understood. The Kolodny group explains: "An injection of morphine almost magically alleviated symptoms, pleasing doctors and patients."

Andrew Kolodny et al., "The Prescription Opioid and Heroin Crisis: A Public Health Approach to an Epidemic of Addiction," *Annual Review of Public Health*, January 2015. www.annualreviews.org.

The highest quantities are prescribed in Alabama, Tennessee, and West Virginia (in that order), whereas Hawaii, California, and New York have the lowest rate of opioid prescriptions.

Examples of opioid painkillers include hydrocodone (brand name Vicodin), oxycodone (OxyContin, Percocet), morphine (Kadian, Avinza), and codeine. According to the National Institute on Drug Abuse (NIDA), hydrocodone products are commonly prescribed for a variety of painful conditions, including pain resulting from injuries and related to dental problems. Morphine is typically used before and after surgical procedures to help ease a patient's severe pain, and codeine may be prescribed for patients whose moderate pain is not alleviated with over-the-counter painkillers.

For people who suffer from severe pain, painkillers can make the difference between being able to function and living in constant agony. This is true of New York City actress Leslie Kendall Dye, whose great passion is ballet. "Ballet has long been my portal to a happier place," she says. "While dancing I can keep my head in the clouds and my feet firmly connected to the ground." In 2009, while Dye was doing a split jump she had done countless times before, a major ligament in her hip ripped in two. The pain was unbearable; she describes it as "white, searing hot agony," adding that "sometimes I thought I might be hallucinating, the pain was so bad."[9] Dye underwent surgery, and after a long period of recovery she was healed enough to return to dancing. But even now, years after her surgery, she still suffers from lingering pain. Some days are worse than others, and when the pain gets unbearable she takes an opioid painkiller called tramadol. Dye has accepted that she may have to cope with pain for the rest of her life, and she can handle that as long as she can live normally and continue pursuing her passion.

Painkiller Use Versus Abuse

Because of the risks involved with opioids, Dye's pain management doctor regularly cautions her about taking tramadol. She understands the risks and takes the drug only when she absolutely needs it. Research has shown this to be true of most people who take painkillers; they use the drugs according to their doctor's recommendations. "Ninety-seven percent of patients don't have a problem with opioids,"[10] says Karsten Kueppenbender, an addiction psychia-trist at Harvard Medical School's McLean Hospital. An April 2015 survey by the Partnership for Drug-Free Kids found that only 7 percent of chronic pain patients and 13 percent of acute (sudden onset or short-term) pain patients had abused their opioid medications.

> "Ninety-seven percent of patients don't have a problem with opioids."[10]
>
> —Karsten Kueppenbender, an addiction psychiatrist at Harvard Medical School's McLean Hospital.

Use of Painkillers Second Only to Marijuana

Health officials emphasize that painkiller abuse is a serious and growing problem in the United States. According to the Substance Abuse and Mental Health Services Administration, current abuse of painkillers (meaning nonmedical use, or use of the drugs not in accordance with a doctor's recommendations) is surpassed only by marijuana use.

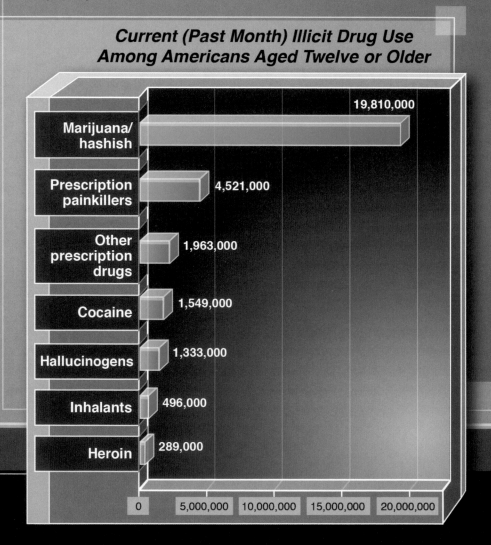

Current (Past Month) Illicit Drug Use Among Americans Aged Twelve or Older

Drug	Number
Marijuana/hashish	19,810,000
Prescription painkillers	4,521,000
Other prescription drugs	1,963,000
Cocaine	1,549,000
Hallucinogens	1,333,000
Inhalants	496,000
Heroin	289,000

0   5,000,000   10,000,000   15,000,000   20,000,000

Source: Substance Abuse and Mental Health Services Administration, "Substance Use and Mental Health Estimates from the 2013 National Survey on Drug Use and Health: Overview of Findings," *NSDUH Report*, September 4, 2014. www.samhsa.gov.

As promising as such findings are, however, health officials still refer to opioid painkillers as the most abused class of drugs in the United States. In fact, prescription drug abuse is considered America's fastest-growing drug problem. In terms of prescription drugs, *abuse* means that the drugs are used in ways (or amounts) that are different from what the prescribing doctor intended. For instance, taking painkillers solely for the feelings they produce, even when not in pain, is an example of painkiller abuse. Another example is taking medication that was prescribed for someone else. "Prescription drug abuse or problematic use," says the Mayo Clinic, "includes everything from taking a friend's prescription painkiller for your backache to snorting or injecting ground-up pills to get high."[11]

NIDA director Nora D. Volkow often speaks publicly about painkiller abuse, referring to it as a serious, pressing public health issue. According to Volkow, NIDA research has shown that nearly 2 million Americans were regular abusers of painkillers during 2013. A 2014 report by the Substance Abuse and Mental Health Services Administration revealed that among Americans aged twelve and older, prescription painkillers were second only to marijuana in prevalence of illicit drug abuse. Volkow offers a number of reasons for these alarming statistics. "The number of prescriptions for some of these medications has increased dramatically since the early 1990s," she says. "Moreover, a consumer culture amenable to 'taking a pill for what ails you' and the perception of prescription drugs as less harmful than illicit drugs are other likely contributors to the problem."[12]

> "Prescription drug abuse ... includes everything from taking a friend's prescription painkiller for your backache to snorting or injecting ground-up pills to get high."[11]
>
> —Mayo Clinic, a world-renowned health care facility headquartered in Rochester, Minnesota.

Most Likely to Abuse

As with many types of substance abuse, painkiller abuse is not unique to any one type of person or group; it affects all kinds of people, regardless of gender, race, ethnicity, religion, or social status. There are, however, risk factors that make certain people more susceptible to abusing the drugs. According to research by Jamison and Mao, a major risk factor is having a personal history and/or family history of substance abuse. Also vulnerable are people who suffer from mental health disorders such as major depression or anxiety disorders; those with a history of physical and/or sexual abuse; and people who have experienced childhood trauma. Jamison and Mao's July 2015 report also cites personality as a risk factor; for instance, individuals with a positive, cheerful nature are not as likely to abuse painkillers as those who suffer from negative emotions and moods.

Identifying risk factors for painkiller abuse is an important step in determining which individuals are most likely to move from short-term use of opioids to long-term abuse. This was the focus of a study led by Mayo Clinic anesthesiologist W. Michael Hooten. For a July 2015 report, Hooten and his colleagues tracked nearly three hundred patients from Olmsted County, one of the largest counties in Minnesota. Each patient had been prescribed opioid painkillers for the first time between January 1 and December 31, 2009. Hooten's group found that people with histories of drug abuse had a significantly higher risk of long-term opioid abuse than those without such a history. Another finding was that past or current smokers were more likely to abuse opioids than non-smokers.

As for why this association occurs, Hooten theorizes that nicotine or other drugs may have the same effects on the brain as opioid painkillers. Because of this, it is important that patients learn to recognize the potential risks associated with these drugs and avoid them if possible. He adds that further research will focus on the potential role of dose and quantity of opioid painkillers: "It is possible that higher dose or greater quantities of the drug with each prescription are important predictors of longer-term use."[13]

Painkiller Abuse Among Youth

Even though painkiller abuse affects people of all ages, health officials are especially concerned about the growing number of adolescents who abuse the drugs. "Youth are increasingly at risk, especially with opioids available in the medicine cabinets of so

A Devastated Region

In the southernmost part of West Virginia, tucked into a wooded hollow in the Appalachian Mountains, lies rural McDowell County. It is home to dozens of communities whose names are indicative of the industry that once boomed there: Coalwood, Coaldale, Coal City, and Coalton. But as Appalachia's coal supply has been exhausted and mining jobs have steadily declined, the region has sunk into poverty, despair, and drug addiction. "Not surprisingly," says Karen Sodomick, who is from West Virginia, "many residents have turned to drug abuse and to the drug trade." Sodomick, who is with the Phoenix House drug treatment program, says that although methamphetamine was Appalachia's biggest problem in the past, "it is clear that prescription opiates are now an ever graver threat."

The statistics of McDowell County are dismal. Fatal painkiller overdoses are more than eight times the national average. In 2011 nearly one out of every three babies born in the local hospital was exposed to these drugs in the womb. "We don't hear about this tragedy as often as we should," says Sodomick. "The news media has preferred instead to focus on the rising problem of prescription drug and heroin addiction in middle-class suburban communities. The people of McDowell, where shanties dot the secluded mountainous landscape, are largely forgotten."

Karen Sodomick, "Fighting Addiction in Appalachia," Phoenix House, April 29, 2014. www.phoenixhouse.org.

many homes,"[14] says the Hazelden Betty Ford Institute for Recovery Advocacy. The NIDA's primary method of gauging health-risk behaviors of American high school students is its Monitoring the Future survey, which has been conducted since 1975. The 2015 survey found that more than 3 percent of high school seniors had abused OxyContin within the past year, and nearly 5 percent had abused Vicodin. The positive news is that these numbers are lower than shown in the 2013 survey. Health officials are still troubled, however, that tens of thousands of American teenagers are abusing opioid painkillers.

Because of the high prevalence of painkiller abuse among youth, a decision by the US Food and Drug Administration (FDA) drew sharp criticism from numerous medical professionals and addiction specialists. In August 2015 the FDA approved the prescription of OxyContin to children as young as age eleven. This approval was limited to young patients with cancer or other diseases that involve severe pain that cannot be effectively treated with other medications. Among those who have spoken out against the FDA's action was New York psychiatrist and addiction expert Andrew Kolodny, who cofounded the advocacy group Physicians for Responsible Opioid Prescribing. "There really aren't many people that are applauding this decision,"[15] he says. Kolodny is not completely against prescribing opioid painkillers for youth, but he believes it should be limited to end-of-life care for those who suffer from terminal illnesses.

Others, however, have a very different point of view. One example is Kathleen A. Neville, who not only supports the FDA's decision—she applauds it. Neville is a pediatric oncologist (children's cancer specialist) at Arkansas Children's Hospital in Little Rock, Arkansas. She treats children with diseases such as cancer or sickle-cell anemia, both of which involve severe, unrelenting pain. Neville has seen firsthand how much her young patients suffer because of that pain, and she is adamant that opioid painkillers should be available to them. "Just because OxyContin has been abused or prescribed inappropriately doesn't mean we should deprive the children who need the drug,"[16] she says.

> "Many abusers of opioid pain relievers are going directly to doctors for their drugs."[18]
>
> —Thomas Frieden, director of the CDC.

Who Supplies Painkillers?

Most people who take painkillers for legitimate medical conditions get prescriptions from a family doctor or pain management specialist. For those who use the drugs nonmedically (thereby abusing them), there are a number of sources from which they may get painkillers. In a practice called doctor shopping, people visit a variety of doctors and/or dentists or travel to emergency rooms in different cities or states to get prescriptions. Or, says Emory University School of Law professor Joanna Shepherd, "a few rogue

Many young people abuse opioids like OxyContin because the drugs can be found in home medicine cabinets. A 2015 decision by the FDA that allowed doctors to prescribe OxyContin for young children drew criticism from some antidrug-abuse advocates who cited the dangers of making the drugs even more accessible.

physicians and pharmacists, lured by substantial profits, enable drug abusers by illegally prescribing or supplying controlled substances." Shepherd says that even the most ethical physicians rarely have adequate training to recognize and address prescription drug abuse. As a result, they "prescribe painkillers to patients who are not using them for legitimate medical purposes."[17]

The sources for people who abuse painkillers often vary based on the extent of their abuse. According to a March 2014 report by Centers for Disease Control and Prevention (CDC) researchers, nearly two-thirds of those who abused painkillers less than thirty days out of the year got the drugs free from their friends or relatives. But the same was not true of those who abused painkillers for two hundred or more days a year; their primary source, according to the study, was most often a physician. "Many abusers of opioid pain relievers are going directly to doctors for their drugs,"[18] says CDC director Thomas Frieden. Other sources for the heaviest painkiller users included buying the drugs from friends, relatives, or a dealer.

One fact that is highly disturbing to health officials and addiction specialists is that people can order almost any drug they want, including painkillers, online. Secretive Internet marketplaces, which are collectively known as the Dark Web, are not reachable through Google or other search engines; those who buy from them must use special browser software to access the sites. According to the watchdog group LegitScript, which tracks online pharmacies, there are from forty thousand to fifty thousand of these illegal online sellers in operation today. LegitScript founder John Horton says it is "disturbingly easy to find a rogue Internet pharmacy that will sell you a prescription drug without a prescription. Research shows that 97 percent of Internet pharmacies are not operating legitimately and most of those do not require a prescription at all."[19]

> "The term 'silent epidemic' sometimes gets overused in medicine. But, for prescription opioid drugs, the term fits disturbingly well."[21]
>
> —Francis Collins, director of the National Institutes of Health.

The "Silent Epidemic"

Opioid painkiller abuse is a serious, fast-growing problem in the United States, and it is disturbing to health officials. "This issue has become a public health epidemic," says Volkow, "with devastating consequences."[20] In most cases people who suffer from severe pain do not abuse the drugs they take; they obtain them legitimately and use them as directed—but this is not true of everyone. Thus, painkiller abuse has soared in recent years to become America's fastest-growing drug problem. "The term 'silent epidemic' sometimes gets overused in medicine," says Collins. "But, for prescription opioid drugs, the term fits disturbingly well."[21]

CHAPTER 2: What Are the Effects of Painkillers?

In 1973 pharmacologist Candace Pert made a profound discovery, one that vastly improved scientific understanding of how opioids relieve pain. For several years she had been curious about the painkilling properties of opioids, starting when she was given morphine for pain after breaking her back. Pert began to speculate about why the drug worked as it did; specifically, how it interacted with the brain and the rest of the nervous system to dull the effects of pain.

In a laboratory at Johns Hopkins University School of Medicine, Pert conducted experiments in which she observed how the brains of rats reacted to opioids such as morphine. In the process, she identified opioid receptors, which are tiny proteins on the surfaces of nerve cells (neurons). With this discovery, Pert's question about morphine's painkilling properties was answered. She now knew that the drug altered someone's perception of pain by binding to opioid receptors in the brain, spinal cord, and other nervous system tissue.

Natural Painkillers

As enthusiastic as Pert was about the discovery, it made her more curious than ever. The receptors obviously existed for a reason; did the brain produce an opioid-like substance that would bind to them? This seemed to be the only plausible explanation, as Pert said in an interview with *Smithsonian* magazine: "God presumably did not put an opiate receptor in our brains so that we could ultimately discover how to get high with opium."[22] Yet even though Pert was confident that such a chemical existed, she was unable to identify it. Eventually, she abandoned her search for the elusive substance and focused her research in other directions.

Scientists worldwide were determined to keep searching for it, however, and in 1975 Scottish researchers succeeded. Hans W. Kosterlitz and John Hughes, from the University of Aberdeen in Scotland, discovered an amino-acid molecule they named en-kephalin, from a Greek term meaning "in the head." Kosterlitz and Hughes had found the molecule during experiments with guinea pigs and mice and learned that it had morphine-like qualities. Later studies revealed that enkephalin was not the only endogenous (naturally oc-curring) chemical with painkilling prop-erties. Rather, it was part of a group of endogenous chemicals produced by the central nervous system and pitu-itary gland. As Pert and other research-ers had long suspected, these natural opioids bind to opioid receptors. Collectively, the painkilling substances are known as endorphins, a term that combines *endogenous* and *morphine*.

> "God presumably did not put an opiate receptor in our brains so that we could ultimately discover how to get high with opium."[22]
>
> —Candace Pert, a pharmacologist who discovered opioid receptors in 1973.

In the years since those important discoveries were made, sci-entists have learned a great deal about the body's natural painkill-ing ability. Studies have revealed, for instance, that the primary triggers for the release of endorphins are pain and stress. Once endorphins have been released, they travel through the blood-stream until they reach opioid receptors, and then bind to them. "Once attached," says the pain advocacy group National Alliance of Advocates for Buprenorphine Treatment (NAABT), "they send signals to the brain of the 'opioid effect' which blocks pain, slows breathing, and has a general calming and anti-depressing effect."[23]

Along with blocking pain signals, when endorphins bind to receptors, they trigger the release of dopamine. This is one of the neurotransmitters, or chemical messengers that pass infor-mation (via rapid-fire electrochemical signals) from one neuron to the next across tiny gaps known as synapses. All neurotransmit-ters have their own specific functions. Dopamine, for instance, is often called the "feel-good" chemical because it helps control the regions of the brain involved in reward and pleasure. It also aids

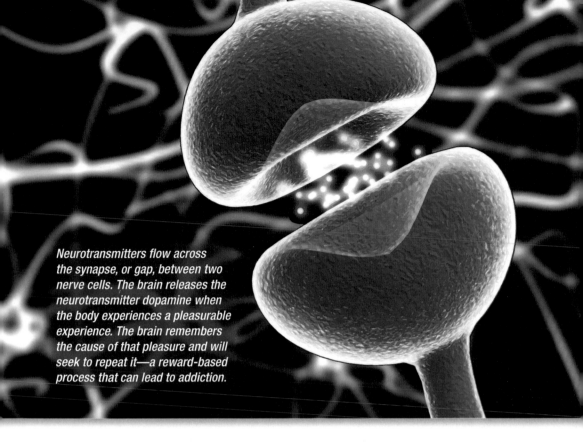

Neurotransmitters flow across the synapse, or gap, between two nerve cells. The brain releases the neurotransmitter dopamine when the body experiences a pleasurable experience. The brain remembers the cause of that pleasure and will seek to repeat it—a reward-based process that can lead to addiction.

in the control of movement, memory, motivation, and emotional responses. When dopamine has been released into the bloodstream, the brain notes that something good has happened and should be remembered. This, according to the NAABT, entices people to repeat whatever it was that caused these pleasant feelings "again and again, without thinking about it."[24]

An Unnatural High

A similar process takes place when people take opioid painkillers. The drugs' chemical structure mimics that of endorphins, so they bind to the same receptors as their endogenous counterparts. This binding blocks pain signals and triggers the release of dopamine. But in stark contrast to the natural release, opioids flood the brain with dopamine, producing far more than people need. Even more than with natural painkillers, the brain remembers the feeling produced by dopamine and compels the user to repeat the behavior that caused it.

When Painkillers Cause Pain

People throughout the world have found that opioid pain medications can bring relief from severe pain. Many experts emphasize, however, that these drugs are not intended for long-term use; rather, they should be taken for no longer than three or four months. There are a number of risks involved if opioids are used for a long time, one of which is a condition known as hyperalgesia. This results from changes in the brain that cause pain to be intensified. Christina Lasich, a physician from Grass Valley, California, explains: "Imagine if a paper cut felt like a red, hot poker stabbed you. Imagine if a small bruise felt like a sledge hammer hit you. If you are able to imagine these examples or maybe have even felt this way, then you know what it is like to have hyperalgesia."

In addition to occurring because of opioid overuse, hyperalgesia can also develop when someone is going through opioid withdrawal. This happens because when the person suddenly discontinues taking opioid pain medication, his or her natural pain-relieving system is dysfunctional, so it cannot kick in and take over. At the same time, the nervous system's pain pathways become extremely reactive, making tissue more sensitive than ever to painful stimuli. "The small hurts hurt even worse," says Lasich. "The minor injuries feel ten times worse. And it seems to hurt everywhere."

Christina Lasich, "Hyperalgesia: It Hurts Everywhere!," HealthCentral, March 2, 2013. www.healthcentral.com.

This is a familiar scenario for a health care professional named David, who began taking painkillers after having his wisdom teeth pulled. He tried taking ibuprofen, but it did not help, and he was in so much pain he felt miserable. So he took Percocet, a prescription painkiller that combines oxycodone and acetaminophen. The memory of that day when he tried the painkiller for the first time is still vivid in his mind. "I can remember exactly where I was standing in the room of my fourth-year medical school student apartment," says David, "the angle of the sun through the windows, where the TV and couch were located. My mind said, 'I don't know what you did, but let's do that again.'"[25]

In addition to the "let's do that again" message, when the brain becomes accustomed to opioid painkillers, it stops producing natural ones. Thus, if someone abruptly stops taking opioids, natural endorphin production does not automatically kick in. "Because we're dependent on our endogenous opioid systems for so much of our daily experience," says alcohol and drug counselor Ian McLoone, "when you tinker with it or stop producing your own endorphins, it affects the whole range of your daily experience."[26] Without opioids or naturally-produced endorphins, withdrawal occurs—and it can be unbearable for the sufferer. Symptoms range from unpleasant to unbearable and include restlessness, insomnia, and diarrhea, as well as elevated blood pressure and heartbeat, uncontrollable shaking, and deep bone and joint pain.

A Wide Range of Side Effects

People who take painkillers for prolonged periods may suffer from a number of side effects, one of which is depression. One study that found a strong link between depression and opioid use was led by St. Louis, Missouri, researcher Jeffrey F. Scherrer. The study, which was released in March 2014, focused on a large group of veterans who were prescribed opioids for pain and who had no history of clinical depression. Scherrer's group found that the risk of depression increased significantly the longer patients took opioid painkillers. For example, patients taking opioids for 90 to 180 days had a 25 percent increased risk of depression. For those who took the drugs for more than 180 days, the risk was higher than 50 percent. "The term 'Pharmageddon' was coined to capture the epidemic nature and adverse public health consequences of opioid analgesics," the study's authors write. "Our findings add to such concerns by showing that opioid use for more than 90 days significantly increases the risk of developing depression."[27]

"Because we're dependent on our endogenous opioid systems for so much of our daily experience, when you tinker with it or stop producing your own endorphins, it affects the whole range of your daily experience."[26]

—Ian McLoone, a drug and alcohol counselor from St. Paul, Minnesota.

A number of other side effects are also associated with opioid painkillers. One risk is hormonal imbalance, meaning lower-than-normal levels of testosterone (male sex hormone) or estrogen (female sex hormone); weakened immune system, which compromises the body's ability to fight off infection and disease; low blood pressure, which can cause dizziness, nausea, and cold, clammy skin; and insomnia. According to Benjamin Abraham, a physician with Cleveland Clinic's Department of Pain Management, "These side effects are not limited to people who abuse opioids or have been taking opioids long-term. They can occur in anybody—even patients who just started an opioid regimen."[28] Because of the numerous risks of taking opioid painkillers, Abraham and many other physicians warn that the drugs should be taken only if absolutely necessary.

> "These side effects are not limited to people who abuse opioids or have been taking opioids long-term. They can occur in anybody—even patients who just started an opioid regimen."[28]
>
> —Benjamin Abraham, a physician with Cleveland Clinic's Department of Pain Management.

According to the Cleveland Clinic, one of the most common side effects of opioid use is constipation. Some patients become constipated almost immediately, within a day or two of taking painkillers. If constipation continues without treatment, complications may range from hemorrhoids to bowel disorders. One of the latter is a painful condition known as narcotic bowel syndrome, in which bowel function slows down. Along with chronic constipation, this can result in periodic or chronic abdominal pain. Narcotic bowel syndrome has also been associated with nausea, bloating, vomiting, and/or abdominal distention (swollen abdomen). The International Foundation for Functional Gastrointestinal Disorders calls narcotic bowel syndrome a serious medical issue that remains underrecognized. "Narcotics have a role in medical care," the foundation explains, "but there are times where the risks outweigh the benefits."[29]

Organ Damage

Among the greatest potential dangers of prolonged use of painkillers is harm to the vital organs, including the lungs. The effect of these drugs is to decrease the breathing rate, which can interfere with the lungs' normal function. In some people who have taken opioid pain-killers for a long time, this can lead to a higher-than-average risk of developing pneumonia. This is especially dangerous for older adults because pneumonia can be deadly. According to an investigation by researchers from the University of Washington, patients taking long-lasting opioid painkillers are more than three times as likely to develop pneumonia as those not taking opioids. "Our results," says lead researcher Sascha Dublin, "mean that it is crucial to look more closely at opioid prescriptions and infections."[30]

Long-term use of opioids can also put the liver at risk. Health officials say this is primarily associated with opioid painkilling drugs that contain high amounts of acetaminophen. As a precau-tionary measure, in 2011 the FDA asked manufacturers to limit the amount of acetaminophen in combination painkillers to 325 milligrams per pill, but surveys have shown that many people take much higher doses than are recommended. This can be deadly, as the FDA explains: "Overdose from prescription combination products containing acetaminophen account for nearly half of all cases of acetaminophen-related liver failure in the United States; many of which result in liver transplant or death."[31] The FDA says that most cases of severe liver damage have occurred in patients who took more than one acetaminophen-containing drug at the same time, exceeded the recommended dosage within a twenty-four-hour period, or drank alcohol while taking the drugs.

Born Suffering

The risks are also great for pregnant women because opioid pain-killers can potentially harm their fetus. According to NIDA direc-tor Nora D. Volkow, one of these risks is for babies to be born with opioid withdrawal, which is symptomatic of a condition called neonatal abstinence syndrome. Volkow says that the condition in-creased by nearly 300 percent in the United States between 2000 and 2009. "This increase," she says, "was driven in part by the high rate of opioid prescriptions being given to pregnant women."[32]

A 2014 study by the American Society of Anesthesiologists examined the prevalence of opioid use among pregnant women.

The extended use of painkillers can pose health risks to the user. However, pregnant women who use these drugs can also unintentionally pass problems on to their fetuses. When they are born, these infants may suffer neonatal abstinence syndrome and go through difficult withdrawal.

The researchers found that more than 14 percent of pregnant women in the United States were prescribed opioids for pain at some point during their pregnancy between 2005 and 2011. Although most of these prescriptions were for short-term pain treatment (less than a week), 2.2 percent of the women were prescribed painkillers more than three times during their pregnancy. The most common complaint was back pain, followed by abdominal pain, migraine headaches, joint pain, and fibromyalgia. At the conclusion of the study, anesthesiologist Edward A. Yaghmour stated that pain during pregnancy is common, and physicians need to carefully balance medications that help the mother with the risks to the unborn. "For example," says Yaghmour, "we would never stop giving anti-seizure medication or medication for diabetes; the danger in those situations is clear. With opioids, there are simply not enough data to have a clear answer. Untreated severe pain in the mother may also be harmful to the fetus."[33]

Health care professionals at Tufts Medical Center in Boston, Massachusetts, have become concerned about the growing number of infants born with neonatal abstinence syndrome. One baby boy was in the hospital for three weeks receiving treatment for opioid withdrawal. His mother had become hooked on Percocet when she was seventeen years old and had struggled with opioid abuse for more than a decade. "When you look at these babies it can break your heart," says Jonathan Davis, chief of newborn medicine at Tufts, "because they are very, very irritable, inconsolable, they are crying, they have tremors." Davis goes on to say that the problem is growing rapidly, and that he and his fellow health care providers are "very, very concerned."[34]

Chasing the Dragon

A common and potentially dangerous side-effect of heavy painkiller use is known as tolerance. This is what occurs when people have used opioids repeatedly and for so long that their brain has stopped responding to the drug as it previously did. As a result, higher and higher doses are needed in order to achieve that same pain-relieving effect. Addiction expert Marvin D. Seppala writes: "Prolonged use of increasingly higher doses of opioids changes the brain so that it functions more or less normally when the drug is present and abnormally when the drug is removed."[35]

The slang term for taking more and more of a drug in a futile effort to achieve the same effects as before is "chasing the dragon." Ironically, euphoria is the effect that most users are chasing when they take opioid painkillers; yet euphoria is the effect most likely to fade away with regular use of opioids. "The opioid receptors have changed at a cellular level," says Seppala, "to protect themselves from overstimulation."[36]

People of all ages have been shown to abuse painkillers, and the number of overdose deaths has soared in recent years. As shown here, those most likely to die by overdose are adults in their mid-forties to mid-fifties.

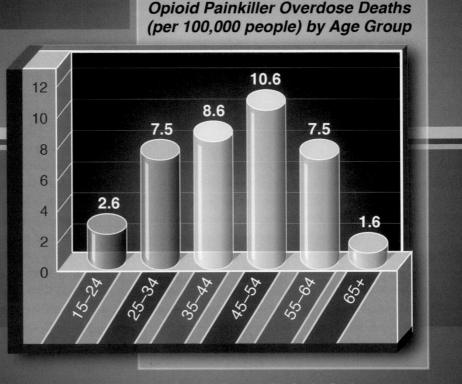

Opioid Painkiller Overdose Deaths (per 100,000 people) by Age Group

Source: Centers for Disease Control and Prevention, "Prescription Drug Overdose Data," October 16, 2015. www.cdc.gov.

Betty Tully, a woman from Chicago, Illinois, quickly developed tolerance for OxyContin. For years she had suffered from a degenerative back condition that caused excruciating pain in her lower back. She visited her doctor, and he encouraged her to try the drug, saying it would relieve her pain without risk of addiction or other negative side effects. Tully decided to give it a try. At first the drug worked as her doctor promised, but it soon became less and less effective. So her doctor increased the dosage—and then increased it again. After only seven months Tully was taking 280 milligrams per day. "That's the equivalent of 56 Percocets a day," she says. When she consulted with a new doctor, he balked at refilling her prescription. "My body was screaming for the drug," says Tully. "My brain was screaming for it."[37]

The Ultimate Danger

Tully was eventually weaned from painkillers, so her story ended well. Unfortunately, that is not true for everyone who develops a tolerance for opioids. The reason tolerance is so dangerous is that it is often a first step toward painkiller overdose—and the incidence of such overdoses has soared in recent years. According to the CDC, the overdose rate in the United States has more than tripled since 1999. Every day one hundred Americans die from drug overdose, and three-quarters of those deaths are from prescription painkillers. Overdose is particularly a risk for

The Myth of "Risk-Free" Painkillers

When health officials warn about the dangers of painkiller abuse, they are typically referring to opioids. But over-the-counter painkillers also come with risks. In fact, in July 2015 the FDA issued a warning about NSAID painkillers, which are available over the counter and in stronger doses by prescription. These include ibuprofen (such as Advil, Motrin, and Children's Motrin), Aleve, Celebrex, and numerous others (aspirin, which is also an NSAID, was not included in the warning).

An expert panel convened by the FDA found that nonaspirin NSAIDs elevated a person's risk of heart attack and stroke. The risk was found to be highest among people who take the drugs at higher doses and for longer periods. Sanjay Kaul, a Los Angeles, California, cardiologist who served on the panel, says that painkillers are widely used, often for "little aches and pains" that do not justify taking pain medication. "The point of this warning is that we have to be very careful," says Kaul. "There has to be a good reason to take them. We shouldn't just be using these drugs willy-nilly."

Quoted in Sabrina Tavernise, "Experts Urge Sparing Use of Nonaspirin Painkillers," *New York Times*, July 13, 2015. www.nytimes.com.

someone who stops taking opioids for a while and then resumes using them. "Users who do not realize they have lost their tolerance during periods of abstinence may initially take the high dosages that they previously had used before quitting,"[38] says Volkow. If they do, she cautions, they are likely to overdose on the drug.

> "My body was screaming for the drug. My brain was screaming for it."[37]
>
> —Betty Tully, a woman from Chicago, Illinois, who developed a tolerance for the painkiller OxyContin.

When people hear about someone dying of an opioid overdose, many automatically assume that the cause of death was an extraordinarily high amount of the drug. Although this is a logical conclusion, it is only partially true. The actual cause of death is respiratory failure—the breathing slows down and becomes more shallow, and the person loses consciousness and often dies within minutes. "Basically, opioids kill via respiratory depression," says science journalist and recovered addict Maia Szalavitz. "They make you go to sleep and forget to breathe."[39]

Because of the overdose risk and the countless other dangers associated with opioid painkillers, a growing number of physicians are discouraging their patients from taking the drugs. Says neurosurgeon and journalist Sanjay Gupta:

> As a doctor, I will look my patients in the eye every time I hand them a prescription to tell them the concerns about the pills they will take. It won't just be a casual reminder . . . but a forceful warning backed up with scary but forceful statistics. I will remind them that they could become addicted, and they could die. That is our jobs as doctors, and it is one way to save thousands of lives.[40]

CHAPTER 3: How Addictive Are Painkillers?

By the time she was nineteen years old, Brittany Ringersen was a hard-core painkiller addict. She barely resembled the happy and energetic teen who, just a few years before, had been an honors student who loved painting, playing basketball, and bicycling with her dad. Now all she cared about was the drugs, how they made her feel, and how soon she could take more of them.

Ringersen's problem had started innocently enough three years before. She had her wisdom teeth removed, and the orthodontist gave her a prescription for Percocet, which he explained would help relieve her pain when the anesthetic wore off. He assured Ringersen that she should be pain-free in about a week, and she was—but she had become very fond of Percocet. She had come to like the warm, drowsy feeling that came over her whenever she took it, and she wanted that to continue. Since she still had some pills left in the bottle, she decided to use them up. She popped one in her mouth and swallowed it with a glass of water, and sure enough, the feeling she had enjoyed washed over her again. "That single, seemingly innocent, just-for-fun pill led to another, and then another," says author Elizabeth Foy Larsen. "And before she even realized it, Brittany didn't just want the drug—she needed it to get out of bed in the morning."[41]

Addiction Explained

What happened to Ringersen is characteristic of addiction. Over time, as she continued taking painkillers, changes occurred in her brain chemistry that caused her to need the drugs just to be able to function. This desperate need is typified in the etymology of the word *addiction*, which comes from a Latin term for *enslaved by* or *bound to*. The need for drugs (as opposed to merely wanting them) is also why most addiction experts define addiction as a complex disease of the brain. People who are addicted to opioids habitually use them without regard for the harmful consequences to themselves or others. In other words, addiction blots out rational thinking and solid reasoning. As the NIDA explains: "Brain imaging studies of drug-addicted individuals show changes in areas of the brain that are critical to judgment, decision making, learning and memory, and behavior control. Together, these changes can drive an abuser to seek out and take drugs compulsively despite adverse, even devastating consequences—that is the nature of addiction."[42]

The perception of addiction has vastly changed since the early- to mid-twentieth century, even among mental health professionals and addiction experts. Researchers first began studying addictive behavior during the 1930s, when the widespread belief was that those who became addicts were bereft of morals or simply lacked the willpower necessary to resist temptation. The authors of a Harvard Medical School publication write: "Overcoming addiction, [people] thought, involved punishing miscreants or, alternately, encouraging them to muster the will to break a habit."[43] Today the notion that addiction is a moral failing or lack of willpower has been discredited. Although scientists do not always agree on exactly what addiction is, it is widely viewed as a complex, chronic disease that can change the brain's structure as well as function. "Just as cardiovascular disease damages the heart and diabetes impairs the pancreas," the Harvard authors write, "addiction hijacks the brain. This happens as the brain goes through a series of changes, beginning with recognition of pleasure and ending with a drive toward compulsive behavior."[44]

The term *addiction* is often used interchangeably with *dependence*, and though they are related they are not exactly the same. One way to view dependence is like a stepping stone toward becoming a full-fledged addict. Physical dependence occurs when the body has adapted to the drug, requiring more and more of it to achieve the wanted effects. When the drug is taken away, this leads to withdrawal, which can be totally unbearable. To avoid going through withdrawal, the person keeps taking opioids. "This is the common experience of most chronic pain patients who are able to take their opioid medication as prescribed for pain but

Addiction to painkillers can result from the abuse of a needed prescription. Percocet, a commonly prescribed opioid pictured here, is used to relieve pain. The pleasurable narcotic effect of the drug registers in the brain, which might lead the user to chase that pleasure through addictive behavior.

don't develop the uncontrollable compulsion and loss of control," says research scientist and addiction expert Charles P. O'Brien. "A desire to avoid withdrawal is not addiction."[45] In essence, someone who is dependent on painkillers is not necessarily addicted (yet), whereas those who are addicted are so highly dependent on the drugs, with such uncontrollable cravings, that they engage in destructive behaviors to maintain their addiction.

Young Addicts

Brain studies have shown that adolescents are especially susceptible to addiction. This is largely because adolescents' brains are not fully developed and do not finish developing until sometime in their twenties. The parts of the brain that are last to develop are the frontal lobes, which are involved with rational decision making and behavioral inhibition, such as the ability to control emotions and impulses. "During adolescence, there's imbalance between the fully mature pleasure and reward system and immature executive functions," says Sharon Levy, a pediatrician who directs the Adolescent Substance Abuse Program at Boston Children's Hospital. "So it's like the gas pedal is on full steam and the brakes are not completely developed yet. The very strong behavioral drive for reward makes adolescents more vulnerable to developing addiction, regardless of which substance."[46]

Health officials are concerned about the growing prevalence of opioid painkiller addiction among adolescents. This increase parallels a rise in opioid prescriptions among youth: According to the American Society of Addiction Medicine (ASAM), the number of opioids prescribed to adolescents and young adults has nearly doubled since 1994—and there appears to be no end in sight. Each day, says ASAM, an estimated twenty-five hundred youth in the United States abuse a prescription pain reliever for the first time. Because these drugs are so powerful, a worrisome number of young people who abuse them become addicted.

Addiction experts say this often happens unintentionally and begins with a legitimate need for pain medication. A young person is prescribed a painkiller by a doctor or dentist, finds the feelings it causes desirable, and wants more. This unintentional path to addiction is at the root of the term *accidental addict*. The implication is that much of the responsibility lies with doctors and/or dentists for failing to adequately educate or warn their patients about the addictive potential of opioid painkillers. "The problem," says psychologist Nicholas Kardaras, who specializes in addiction, "often lies within the training that physicians receive, which may be only one day of addiction education during six years of medical school training."[47]

> "Addiction deceives us, letting us think that we can use drugs on our own terms."[48]
>
> —Brittany Ringersen, a recovered painkiller addict from South Florida.

Once Ringersen became hooked on Percocet, she started hanging out with a new crowd of friends who were known for using opioids. They encouraged her to start using Roxicodone pills, which are known as Roxys and are more powerful than Percocet. Within a few months Ringersen had switched from taking pills orally to crushing them up to snort or smoke, and she was doing this several times a day. All the while, she fooled herself into believing that she could stop using whenever she wanted to. "Addiction deceives us," says Ringersen, "letting us think that we can use drugs on our own terms."[48]

Many Patients Not Informed of Addiction Risk

When physicians prescribe opioid painkillers, it is essential that they talk with their patients about the risks, including how addictive the drugs are. Most physicians say they do this; but according to an April 2015 survey by Partnership for Drug-Free Kids, a disturbing number of them do not.

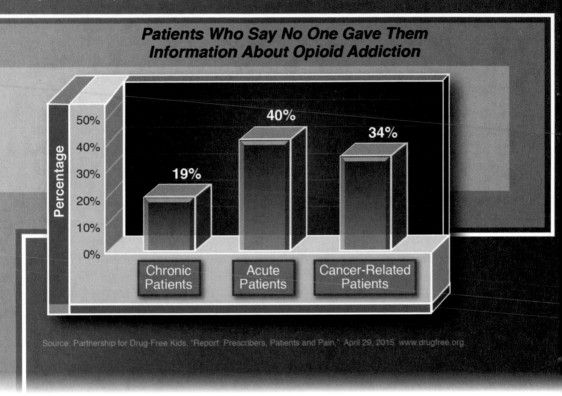

Patients Who Say No One Gave Them Information About Opioid Addiction

Source: Partnership for Drug-Free Kids, "Report: Prescribers, Patients and Pain," April 29, 2015. www.drugfree.org

Highly Addictive Drugs

Opioid painkillers are known to be some of the most addictive drugs. Many people are not aware that chemically, opioids are nearly identical to their illegal cousin, diacetylmorphine, which is better known as heroin. This lack of awareness was revealed during a March 2015 survey by the National Safety Council. Nearly half of opioid painkiller users surveyed had no idea that the drugs they take have chemical makeups that are almost identical to heroin and are just as addictive. Even more striking was that nine out of ten opioid painkiller users were not concerned about addiction at all—and nearly half did not even realize that the painkillers they were taking were opioids. "Americans should not be fooled: an opioid painkiller is the equivalent of legal heroin," says National

Safety Council president Deborah A.P. Hersman. "The drugs in our medicine cabinets can be just as addictive as illicit ones."[49]

The main reason opioid painkillers are so addictive is what takes place when they attach to receptors in the brain and throughout the body. As pain signals are blocked by this binding and excess dopamine is released, the brain is "tricked" into believing that ingesting opioids is necessary for survival and must be repeated. Marriage and family therapist Lindsay Kramer writes:

> [A] person takes opiates. Opiates release chemicals that bind to the opioid receptors and produce a euphoric feeling. The euphoric feeling is better than the brain expects, so it releases the neurotransmitter dopamine to reward the user for the opiate use, which also causes the user to feel good. . . . More opiates equal more euphoria, which produces more dopamine, which creates a behavioral motivation to continue to use in order to achieve the same effect. It's a vicious cycle of using to feel good, and the good feelings leading back to using.[50]

Opioid addiction is also closely linked to the withdrawal that addicts (recovered and current) experience when they quit taking the drugs. The very thought of going through such a horrible experience is frightening enough for them to continue taking the drugs, no matter what the consequences may be. For these individuals, using painkillers is no longer about the warm sensations, euphoria, or other positive feelings they once experienced. "An addict then is taking his or her drug of (no) choice in order to feel 'normal,' a concept that is difficult to grasp," says addiction expert Marvin D. Seppala. "Many people assume addicts enjoy the daily use of their drugs, but most opioid addicts cannot recall the last time their drug use was enjoyable."[51]

"An opioid painkiller is the equivalent of legal heroin. The drugs in our medicine cabinets can be just as addictive as illicit ones."[49]

—Deborah A.P. Hersman, president of the National Safety Council.

34

Addiction-Proof Painkillers?

One reason it is easy for people to get addicted to opioids is how they take the drugs: crushing pills into a powder and snorting them, or crushing and dissolving them in water and then injecting the liquid. This is true of OxyContin, which is known for time-release effects that last up to twelve hours. If someone snorts or injects the drug, however, its effects hit the person all at once. Health officials say this type of use plays a major role in the soaring opioid addiction and overdose rates in the United States.

Purdue Pharma, the pharmaceutical company that makes OxyContin, has been vilified (and heavily fined) for deliberately misleading the public about the drug's addiction potential. To help rectify this and help reduce OxyContin abuse and addiction, Purdue introduced a formula that made the pills crush proof. A May 2013 *Popular Science* article says that by making the pills "weirdly difficult to crush or dissolve in water," Purdue is hoping to "undercut the ways that people had discovered they could get a super-sized opioid hit from long-lasting OxyContin." A few studies have confirmed that OxyContin's crush-resistant formula could lead to a decline in abuse of the drug, though it remains to be seen if this will reduce painkiller abuse and addiction overall.

Francie Diep, "How Do You Make a Painkiller Addiction-Proof?," *Popular Science*, May 13, 2013. www.popsci.com.

Emily Carter Roiphe, a writer and literary critic, remembers being torn between desperately needing her drug and knowing she had to give it up. When she finally quit, she went through a terrible time with withdrawal. "What's horrible is how badly you miss your drug," she says, "because you know it will give you relief. It's very unpleasant, there's no doubt about it." Roiphe felt weak and sick, suffered from aching joints, and could not relax or sleep at night. "Basically, you just feel like crap," she says. She adds that withdrawal can bring despair; without the emotional numbness induced by painkillers, addicts no longer have a shield to protect them from pain and sorrow. "Then all the emotions come back," says Roiphe. "It's very common to see people weeping over dog-food commercials and such. People are very raw, extremely raw."[52]

Older Addicts

Painkiller addiction affects people of all ages, but certain groups have been shown to have a higher risk than others. According to data from the Agency for Healthcare Research and Quality, the age group with the highest number of hospitalizations for overdose is adults aged forty-five to eighty-five. Between 1993 and 2012 overdoses among people of this age group increased fivefold—and the rate of overdose deaths among the same age group jumped sevenfold. Data from IMS Health, an organization that tracks drug dispensing data for the US government, revealed that 55 million opioid prescriptions were written during 2013 for people aged sixty-five and over, which was a 20 percent increase over five years.

Addiction expert Andrew Kolodny explains that older adults are at high risk for opioid addiction because of the pain they experience with age. "These are individuals who mostly have become addicted to opioids through medical treatment," says Kolodny. "And because they're older, because they tend to have multiple medical problems or suffer from chronic pain, this is a group that can usually get all of the pills they need from doctors."[53] Because addicts are typically assumed to be younger, painkiller addiction among the elderly is often called a "hidden epidemic." In fact, according to Kolodny, people aged forty-five to fifty-four are much more likely to die of overdose than younger people. "In many cases," he says, "these are individuals that are overdosing on pills that were legitimately prescribed to them."[54]

Fortunately, Betty Van Amburgh did not overdose on the painkillers she was taking. But as a woman in her sixties, she exemplifies Kolodny's description of an older person who became addicted. When Van Amburgh started treatment for her problem, she was asked to bring all the medications that she had been taking to the treatment facility. She arrived carrying a shopping bag that was stuffed with a jaw-dropping assortment of boxes and bottles and skin patches. The health care providers who worked at the facility were incredulous. "They kept saying, 'How did you get so much?'"[55] Van Amburgh recalls. She had been taking opioid medications for about twenty years after having back surgery, but she was unaware what taking so many drugs could do to her.

Nor did she ever observe any sort of apprehension or caution on the part of her physicians, including general practitioners, orthopedists, and pain specialists. "The doctors just kept prescribing them," she says. "It was always, 'Do you have pain? Let me give you a prescription.' But I got addicted. I was a zombie."[56]

Gateway to Heroin

One of the most disturbing trends among people who get addicted to painkillers is that so many migrate from those drugs to heroin. According to NIDA director Nora D. Volkow, the incidence of heroin initiation (meaning first time use) is nineteen times higher among people who started by abusing painkillers than among those who did not abuse painkillers. A December 2014 NIDA fact sheet explains that in three separate surveys, nearly half of young people who inject heroin reported abusing prescription opioids first. When people switch, it is invariably because of cost; if they can no longer get prescriptions from their doctor, they find that painkillers can cost fifty dollars per pill or even more when bought from a dealer. "People eventually say, 'Why am I paying $1 per milligram for oxy when for a tenth of the price I can get an equivalent

Health officials worry that the abuse of painkillers is often a gateway to heroin use. Some believe the switch to heroin may be the result of a user's inability to get an opioid prescription renewed. Whatever the reason, studies attest to the fact that many heroin users previously abused painkillers.

dose of heroin?'"[57] says Jason Jerry, an addiction specialist at the Cleveland Clinic's Alcohol and Drug Recovery Center.

This is a familiar scenario for David Mundy, who lives in Fairfax, Virginia, a suburb of Washington, DC. Mundy's best friend, Nick, switched to heroin after getting addicted to painkillers. He tried numerous times to get clean and seemed to be making progress. Then in February 2014 Nick died at his home of a heroin overdose. Mundy created a website to help raise money for Nick's family and

Painkillers from Poison?

Because of opioids' soaring addiction rates, scientists throughout the world are exploring ways to make painkillers that are just as effective, but without the addictive properties. This has been the focus of researchers from Queensland, Australia, who in March 2015 announced they had found a possible source of such a painkiller—venom from some of the deadliest spiders on earth. This venom, which spiders use to paralyze or kill prey, contains molecules that can impair the transmission of pain signals between the nerves and the brain. The researchers believe that painkillers made from this venom would be nonaddictive because venom blocks a specific channel that transmits pain to the brain. This differentiates it from opioid painkillers, which block opioid receptors on cells scattered throughout the body, including the brain, spinal cord, and other organs.

The researchers collected venom from more than two hundred spider species, such as the Borneo orange-fringed tarantula and the greenbottle blue tarantula. Australia is an especially good place to find spiders for this research, as University of Queensland researcher Jennifer Smith explains: "We have a plethora of really good venomous animals: You name it, we've got it, pretty much. Australia is the venom land." Smith, a coauthor of the study, says that about 40 percent of the spider venom collected contained peptides (the building blocks of proteins) capable of blocking pain channels. Although it is too early to know for certain whether spider venom will be used to make nonaddictive painkillers, Smith and her colleagues are excited about their findings.

Quoted in Rachel Pannett, "Scientists Target New Painkillers from Spider Venom," *Wall Street Journal*, April 20, 2015. www.wsj.com.

was overwhelmed by the donations that poured in. But what astounded him the most was the number of text and Facebook messages he received from others whose lives had also been touched by addiction. "Parents telling me their kids have problems, kids telling me their friends have problems," says Mundy. "We started talking to people we knew and they were doing heroin, too. And for every single one, the correlation was OxyContin."[58]

The link between painkiller and heroin use is reflected in the fact that health officials have observed a large increase in heroin overdoses among an unlikely group: high school athletes. In fact, a seven-month investigation by *Sports Illustrated* confirmed the high prevalence of heroin addiction among high school athletes, including players of baseball, basketball, football, golf, hockey, lacrosse, soccer, volleyball, and other sports. For many athletes, this addiction began with an experience of using painkillers to alleviate pain from injuries they sustained during play.

> **"I knew painkillers were not good, but I didn't know how crazy addictive they were."[59]**
>
> —Patrick Trevor, a former high school lacrosse star who became addicted to painkillers and then to heroin.

This is what happened to Patrick Trevor, who was a sophomore in high school when he shattered his right thumb during a lacrosse game. A star goalie, Trevor knew that his future could depend on an athletic scholarship, so all he could think of was getting back out on the field. A team doctor examined him and prescribed Roxicodone, which worked like a charm—until Trevor could not stop taking it. Within a few years he had gone from crushing and snorting Roxys to shooting up heroin.

Trevor found a treatment program that helped him get clean and has not touched any drugs since 2012. He recalls feeling surprised by the number of athletes who were at the same rehab facility, being treated for opioid addiction just like he was. "Hockey, football, lacrosse," he says. "[Heroin is] a big thing in sports." Trevor goes on to say that looking back, he had no idea how powerful opioids were until he was addicted to them. "I knew painkillers were not good," he says, "but I didn't know how crazy addictive they were."[59] Based on the soaring rate of opioid addiction in the United States, tens of thousands of others share Trevor's lack of awareness about how addictive painkillers can be.

Celine Gounder has been concerned about the growth of opioid painkiller use for a number of years. A physician who practices in New York City, Gounder began hearing about the alarming opioid painkiller statistics early in her medical career. She learned, for instance, that the United States (with 5 percent of the world's population) consumes 99 percent of global hydrocodone and 80 percent of oxycodone. This was deeply troubling; at the same time prescription drug usage was soaring, painkiller addiction and overdose rates were rising. Gounder could find no evidence that opioid painkillers were effective over the long term, yet millions of people were taking the drugs for months or even years. Referring to the Hippocratic oath ("first, do no harm"), which all medical students are taught in school, she asks: "How did doctors, who pledge to do no harm, let the use of prescription narcotics get so out of hand?"[60]

Rethinking Pain Treatment

Although it is true that physicians have played a role in the fast growth of prescription painkiller use, that was largely unintentional. Many doctors are unaware of how risky opioid painkillers can be for their patients, as CDC director Thomas Frieden explains: "I think there are a lot of doctors who—like me—weren't trained to have a due respect for just how dangerous these drugs are. They are addictive, and they are highly lethal." Frieden goes on to say that there are times when opioid painkillers are appropriate, but they should be prescribed much more sparingly than they are today. "If you have someone in agony who has just had a car crash, by all means give an opioid," he says. "This can also apply to a patient in pain and dying from pancreatic cancer. But if you have an opiate-naive patient—someone who has never seen opioids—it's a momentous decision to give that patient an opioid. You may be forcing them to embark on a life of addiction."[61]

Patients are not always naive about opiates, however; in fact, they have also played a role in the opioid painkiller problem. Gounder has seen for herself how persistent patients can be when they are in pain and want medications that take the pain away. "Many people believe deeply in the power of modern medicine to cure illness," she says, "and bristle at the notion that pain is a fact of life." Gounder says it can be very difficult to talk patients out of a particular medication they have decided is necessary. "Doctors have a hard time saying no," she says, "whether a patient is asking for a narcotic to relieve pain or an antibiotic for the common cold." She adds, though, that the opioid painkiller crisis has forced physicians to rethink their roles. "Doctors have a duty to relieve suffering," she says, "and many of us became doctors to help people. But giving that help isn't straightforward, especially when it comes to chronic pain."[62]

> "How did doctors, who pledge to do no harm, let the use of prescription narcotics get so out of hand?"[60]
>
> —Celine Gounder, a physician from New York City.

Drug-Free Treatment

With the growing painkiller abuse problem in the United States and the drugs' addictive potential, many physicians are encouraging their patients to manage their pain without drugs. Gounder is an advocate of alternative pain management methods such as acupuncture, physical therapy, massage, and chiropractic therapy. She sees how these pain methods are underutilized, in part because they can be expensive and are not always covered by insurance. Whatever method works best, Gounder says it is essential for health care providers to take their patients' pain seriously and help them manage it—preferably without painkilling drugs. "There are other ways to treat pain,"[63] she says.

Treating pain in ways that do not involve drugs is a concept that Jennifer Matesa fully embraces. But it took a long, agonizing

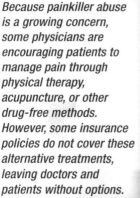

Because painkiller abuse is a growing concern, some physicians are encouraging patients to manage pain through physical therapy, acupuncture, or other drug-free methods. However, some insurance policies do not cover these alternative treatments, leaving doctors and patients without options.

battle with opioid addiction for her to reach that point. After suffering from debilitating pain caused by migraine headaches and fibromyalgia, Matesa visited a pain clinic in Pittsburgh, Pennsylvania. The health care providers at the clinic prescribed a variety of opioid painkillers, including morphine and oxycodone. Matesa took the drugs for six years and finally had to acknowledge that her life had changed radically—and not for the better. "I wasn't treating my pain properly," says Matesa. She eventually stopped going to the pain clinic and hired a private physician to supervise her as she detoxed from opioids. She then began a pain management program that involved exercise (walking and running if she felt up to it), nutritional therapy, adequate sleep every night, and meditation. "By healing myself," she says, "I heal the pain."[64]

A Healing Place

The philosophy that patients must play a role in healing themselves is at the heart of the chronic pain and addiction program at the Betty Ford Center in Rancho Mirage, California. Led by pain management and addiction expert Peter Przekop, the program emphasizes holistic care and healing, rather than blocking pain out by using narcotic drugs. "We look for the underlying cause of the pain," says Przekop. "We treat the brain, not just the pain."[65] In his program, Przekop treats chronic pain patients with a multifaceted approach that includes psychotherapy, exercise, and qigong (pronounced *chi kung*). The latter is an ancient Chinese healing system that integrates movement, physical postures, breathing techniques, and meditation. According to the National Qigong Association, the gentle, rhythmic movements of the practice can reduce stress, build stamina and vitality, and boost the immune system.

> "We treat the brain, not just the pain."[65]
>
> —Peter Przekop, a pain management and addiction expert with the Betty Ford Center in Rancho Mirage, California.

The daily routine for patients in Przekop's program involves spending time each day building awareness of how chronic pain has changed their way of thinking and coping, as well as facing how they have been judging themselves and others. Przekop says that in addition to qigong, patients practice kung fu, tai chi, and yoga. This helps them learn how to refocus their attention while they gain strength, flexibility, and confidence—all methods of staving off chemical dependency while focusing more on natural healing. Another key element of the program is mindfulness exercises. These, according to Przekop, allow patients to "slow down their mind, control their thoughts, and gain a sense of presence. Pain steals this ability from people."[66]

In 2014 the Betty Ford Center released a study of more than two hundred patients (65 percent women and 35 percent men) who had completed Przekop's pain management program. On average, the patients had suffered from chronic pain for fifteen years. More than 90 percent had been prescribed painkillers, and of those, 71 percent admitted taking higher doses than their doctors had prescribed. Nearly all the participants had been using multiple drugs in an effort to cope with their chronic pain, including alcohol in about half of the cases. However, the study revealed that nearly three-fourths of the patients were pain free and substance free a year after their treatment at the clinic ended.

One of these patients was a Native American woman named Jeanian. For many years she struggled with alcoholism and drug abuse. After a horrifying car crash left her with a broken hip, pelvis, leg, and foot, she suffered from pain so severe that she was delusional. She explains: "To deal with the pain, I drank more alcohol, on top of taking prescription oxycodone. I was in a wheelchair. I had reached bottom." In March 2013 Jeanian entered Przekop's pain management program. "It's magical," she says. By the time she had completed the program, she was not dependent on alcohol or drugs, and pain no longer dominated her life. "When I began treatment I walked only indoors, not very far, with a cane. I was mad at the world. By the end of the program I walked up to five miles on paths across the campus."[67]

Attitude Matters

Pain management specialist Charles E. Argoff shares Jeanian's belief in natural healing. A neurology professor at Albany Medical College and director of the school's Comprehensive Pain Center, Argoff emphasizes that how people view their pain can have a profound effect on how they cope with it, as well as their chances of feeling better. He says that sometimes people cannot accept their condition and thus refuse to expend the physical and emotional effort necessary to manage their pain. "Complete pain relief is not reasonable," says Argoff, "nor is expecting to be able to return to the same degree of activity that you had previously. However, you and your doctor can outline meaningful and realistic expectations. If you achieve those goals, look at what more you can do."[68]

In his work with patients, Argoff stresses the importance of exercise in a pain management program, but this is not always met with a positive reaction. Argoff says that many people have an aversion to starting an exercise program and are not interested in doing so. This is especially common among people suffering from chronic pain; they are already hurting, and they fear that exercise will make their pain worse. Research has shown, however, that gentle exercise plans developed by qualified professionals (such as a physical therapist) can actually relieve pain while making the person feel better physically and psychologically. The bottom line, says Argoff, is that people should not feel like they are being controlled by their pain: "Be vigilant, be realistic, and don't give up."[69]

Argoff's perspective is closely related to the importance of having a positive attitude. Pain management experts stress that a person's attitude can potentially make the difference between success or failure in any pain management program. This was revealed during a 2015 study of patients in the United Kingdom who underwent acupuncture for chronic back pain. An ancient Chinese healing method, acupuncture involves inserting extremely thin needles through the skin at strategic points on the body. Research has shown it can

Acupuncture is one alternative method for treating pain. However, a study of back pain patients in the United Kingdom found that the relief patients experienced often corresponded to their willingness or hesitation to believe in the viability and effectiveness of the treatment.

relieve pain from headaches, fibromyalgia, osteoarthritis, and dental surgery, as well as from other sources. The purpose of the study was to find out why some people with chronic back pain gain more benefit from acupuncture than others.

Four hundred eighty-five people who were currently receiving acupuncture for lower back pain participated in the study. A key finding was that the participants' attitudes about themselves and their pain were closely related to whether healing took place. "The analysis showed that psychological factors were consistently associated with back-related disability,"[70] says University of Southampton researcher Felicity Bishop, who led the study. Bishop says that those who started out with low expectations of acupuncture—meaning they thought it would probably not help them—experienced little benefit from the treatment.

How Acupuncture Works

The Chinese healing technique known as acupuncture has existed for three thousand years and is widely recognized as an integral part of pain management. In traditional Chinese medicine, acupuncture is explained as a way to bring the flow of energy (known as chi) back into balance. This is based on an ancient philosophy that describes the universe, and the body, in terms of two opposing forces: yin and yang. When energy is flowing freely and naturally, these life forces are in balance and the body is healthy. But if the energy gets blocked, says the UC San Diego Center for Integrative Medicine, "like water getting stuck behind a dam, the disruption can lead to pain, lack of function, or illness."

Acupuncture involves inserting ultrafine needles through the skin at strategic sites called acupuncture points, or acupoints. This releases blocked chi in the body, which stimulates the body's natural healing response. Some Western practitioners have a different view about why acupuncture is effective. They believe that inserting needles into acupoints stimulates nerves, muscles, and connective tissue, which boosts the body's natural painkillers and increases blood flow.

UC San Diego Center for Integrative Medicine, "How Acupuncture Can Relieve Pain and Improve Sleep, Digestion and Emotional Well-Being," 2015. http://cim.ucsd.edu.

As for the study participants who were enthusiastic about acupuncture and viewed it in a hopeful, positive light, their expectations were met as well. "In particular," says Bishop, "they experienced less disability over the course of treatment when they came to see their back pain as more controllable, when they felt they had better understanding of their back pain, when they felt better able to cope with it, were less emotional about it, and when they felt their back pain was going to have less of an impact on their lives."[71] Bishop says the study's findings hint at how crucial one's attitude is when suffering from pain. She suggests that during the initial consultation, acupuncturists discuss with patients the benefits of thinking more positively about their ability to cope with pain.

The Value of Therapy

In addiction treatment programs such as the one founded by Brittany Ringersen, psychotherapy plays a major role in helping people recover from addiction to painkillers or other drugs. The type of therapy in which they participate varies according to each patient's individual needs. For instance, family therapy can help heal relationships that have broken down because of problems caused by someone's addiction. Family members learn better ways of communicating their own feelings as well as how to listen to each other. In addition to offering support, family members can hold their loved one accountable for sticking with the recommended treatment program, which has been shown to sharply reduce relapse.

For people who struggle with chronic pain and try to manage it without painkillers, cognitive behavioral therapy (CBT) has proved to be effective. The premise of CBT is healthy thinking: stopping negative thoughts when they happen and replacing them with positive, helpful ones. CBT teaches patients to think of pain in a different way so the body and mind are prepared and can respond better when pain strikes. "You may not be able to stop physical pain from happening," says the National Institutes of Health. "But, with practice, you can control how your mind manages the pain. An example is changing a negative thought, such as 'I can't do anything anymore,' to a more positive thought, such as 'I dealt with this before and I can do it again.'"[72]

A 2013 study led by psychiatrist and neuroscientist Magdalena Naylor found that CBT can physically change the brain structure of patients with chronic pain. Scientists know that the human brain is malleable and can be shaped by powerful experiences such as chronic pain. Prior research has shown that the brains of people who live with pain have reduced gray matter, or the outermost portion of the brain that houses its intricate communication network. Naylor's study revealed that the brains of patients who participated in CBT showed an increase in gray matter. "I think this gives me and other physicians and psychologists ammunition to recommend this kind of treatment," she says. "It's not only clinical, but those clinical outcomes are correlated with physical changes in the brain."[73] Scientists are encouraged by this finding, since it is one more indication of how beneficial CBT can be for patients with chronic pain.

Medication-Assisted Treatment

One therapy method that has a proven success rate with people addicted to opioid painkillers is known as maintenance therapy. This approach, which has widespread support among health officials and addiction specialists, involves treating patients with drugs known as opioid antagonists. Like painkillers, these drugs bind to opioid receptors in the brain—but unlike painkillers, opioid antagonists do not activate the receptors. The thinking behind this treatment approach is that much like diabetes or high blood pressure, for which sufferers take medication, opioid addiction is also a disease that requires medication to help someone stay drug free. The three most common drugs used in opioid addiction treatment are methadone, buprenorphine, and naltrexone.

Supporters of this treatment approach emphasize that the medications are safe, cost-effective, and valuable components of opioid addiction treatment. But because their use constitutes treating drug addiction with new drugs, the practice is sometimes frowned on. According to Austin Frakt, Boston University School of Public Health professor, maintenance therapy is misunderstood for much the same reason as addiction. "Culturally," says Frakt, "there's a temptation to view dependency as a result of poor life-

Methadone is one opioid antagonist used in the treatment of painkiller addiction. Opioid antagonists bind to neural receptors in the same way that opioids do, but they do not provide the euphoric rush of those drugs. Thus, methadone helps addicts reduce drug tolerance and fight withdrawal.

style choices, not as a chronic disease, and to view maintenance treatment as merely substituting one addiction for another."[74] That viewpoint makes no sense, says Frakt, and shows that people really still lack an understanding of what addiction is.

In his practice, psychiatrist and addiction specialist Charles H. Silberstein uses Suboxone, which is the brand name of buprenorphine. He explains that although it is an opioid, it is very different from painkillers like OxyContin or Vicodin. "Suboxone binds so strongly to the opiate receptor," says Silberstein, "that once an addict is on it, drugs like heroin or oxycontin have minimal, if any, effect. Suboxone lasts a long time, blocks craving, and doesn't typically induce a high."[75] Silberstein only prescribes the drug for patients who participate in his therapy sessions, and he requires random drug screens to make sure patients stay clean. He has seen numerous patients regain control of their lives after taking Suboxone, though they often must hide the fact that they take it

Giving Back

After Brittany Ringersen recovered from painkiller addiction, she wanted to do something to help other women who were still struggling. So in February 2014 she founded an outpatient treatment program called Lighthouse Recovery Institute in Delray Beach, Florida. Each patient's treatment program is individual and unique to her needs and may include meetings with trauma counselors, nutritionists, and eating disorder specialists. Patients also participate in individual psychotherapy and/or in group therapy, where they learn from each other's experience. Also, the women learn about good health practices and life skills that can help them avoid falling into old habits and relapsing. In addition, they are encouraged to participate in exercise and to explore various hobbies and interests, because so often drug addiction has blotted out everything else in their lives. Yoga is offered at the Lighthouse facility, as well as tai chi, art therapy, and other recreational activities and programs.

Ringersen finds it immensely rewarding to see women being transformed as they work through the treatment program. "I get to help spread the message that I never heard about the dangers of prescription drugs," she says, "as well as the fact that recovery is possible." So many patients arrive at the facility with a sense of defeat, even to the point of not caring if they live or die. By the time they complete their treatment, most of them have a brand new outlook on life, and this fills Ringersen with joy.

Quoted in Elizabeth Foy Larsen, "Good Teens Turned Drug Addicts," *Huffington Post*, September 24, 2014. www.huffingtonpost.com.

because of the negative reactions they encounter from those who are against the drug. "Hopefully," says Silberstein, "the time will come when the judgment toward individuals who need medication for their addictions will fade."[76]

A Promising Test

Health care professionals who share Silberstein's beliefs about maintenance therapy were encouraged by the findings of an April 2015 study. It was conducted by researchers from NYU Langone Medical Center and involved a group of thirty-three male opioid addicts. All the men had been incarcerated in New York City jails, and each consented to participate in the trial. Of those, sixteen were injected with extended-release naltrexone before their release and shortly afterward. The remaining seventeen men did not receive the drug, forming the control group.

One month following their release, 88 percent of the control group relapsed, compared with only 38 percent who took naltrexone. Also, the men in the control group were more likely to be reincarcerated than those who took naltrexone. These findings are encouraging to the researchers, who say that naltrexone shows "substantial benefits" for the treatment of opioid addiction. They explain: "Prisons and jails are ideal environments to offer these treatments and to promote their continued use in the community."[77]

Better Treatment Is Out There

Whether people are struggling with chronic pain, addiction to painkillers, or both, there are many treatment options available to them. Helicopter pilot Darisse Smith is one person who knows from personal experience how difficult it is to live with chronic pain, and also the true and long-term relief that alternative treatments can provide. "There is not one kind of treatment that works for everybody," says Smith, who tried painkillers, surgery, physical therapy, and other types of treatments before getting a surgically

> "If all you are getting for chronic pain is painkillers, you need to find better treatment."[78]
>
> —Darisse Smith, a US Army captain and helicopter pilot.

implanted device that gave her relief. "Chronic pain involves every aspect of your life. If all you are getting for chronic pain is painkillers, you need to find better treatment."[78]

CHAPTER 5: How Can Painkiller Abuse Be Prevented?

In May 2015 agents from the Drug Enforcement Administration (DEA) arrested more than two hundred people during surprise raids of pharmacies, medical centers, and pain clinics. These facilities, located in Arkansas, Alabama, Louisiana, and Mississippi, were well known "pill mills," illegal operations in which doctors prescribe pain pills for profit. The raids were part of a broader DEA operation called Operation Pilluted, which has netted hundreds of arrests, including doctors and pharmacists. "We have people who have taken an oath to do no harm who are throwing that oath out the window,"[79] says DEA special agent Keith Brown.

After raids took place in Montgomery and several other cities in Alabama, Governor Robert Bentley spoke at a press conference. Bentley, who is a physician, held up his medical license and spoke about the responsibilities doctors have to be ethical. He used the words "embarrassment to the medical profession" to describe doctors who were caught during the DEA operation. "When they choose to overprescribe narcotics to patients," says Bentley, "and they know that these patients may be or are abusing them, then they change from being a physician to really being a drug dealer."[80] According to the DEA, efforts such as Operation Pilluted are part of a widespread, aggressive strategy for clamping down on the illegal sale and distribution of opioid painkillers.

Bold Steps by the DEA

Another step toward fighting opioid abuse and addiction was the DEA's 2014 reclassification of hydrocodone combination drugs (hydrocodone plus acetaminophen) such as Vicodin. With 137 million prescriptions in 2013, hydrocodone drugs are the most prescribed painkillers in the United States. "These products are some of the most addictive and potentially dangerous prescription medications available,"[81] says DEA administrator Michele Leonhart. Because of the DEA's action, the painkillers are now on the same schedule (category) as other legal substances (such as morphine) that are known to have the highest potential for abuse, misuse, and/or addiction.

As a result of the rescheduling, people who take hydrocodone need to physically take a prescription to a pharmacy; doctors cannot call or fax in prescriptions for the drugs, as they were able to in the past. The drugs will be limited to a ninety-day supply, and to get more, a new prescription is required. The thinking behind these and other measures is that tougher restrictions will discourage doctors from prescribing opioid painkillers and reduce the chance that patients will become addicted to them. As an addiction expert and president of the advocacy group Physicians for Responsible Opioid Prescribing, Andrew Kolodny was delighted at the DEA's action. He refers to it as the "single most important change that could happen." He shares his thoughts about why the DEA's action was so important: "The best way to treat any

DEA agents lead a suspect away from a medical clinic in Arkansas. The 2015 multistate raids on "pill mills" nabbed doctors and pharmacists who were believed to be prescribing or dispensing pain medications for illegal profit. Authorities noted that overprescription is as problematic as abuse.

disease, whether it's Ebola or opioid addiction, is to stop creating more people with the disease."[82]

One new tool in the DEA's fight against opioid painkiller abuse is an anonymous tip line called TIP411, which was launched in February 2014. Those who have a tip to report can send a text to TIP411 with the keyword *PILLTIP*. The message will be forwarded directly to a DEA agent, who will follow up with an investigation. Georgia is one of the first states to try the new texting program, as health officials and law enforcement in the state are frustrated at how the problem has grown. "It really is out of control here,"[83] says Rick Allen, director of the Georgia Drug and Narcotics Agency.

> "The best way to treat any disease, whether it's Ebola or opioid addiction, is to stop creating more people with the disease."[82]
>
> —Andrew Kolodny, an addiction expert who serves as president of the advocacy group Physicians for Responsible Opioid Prescribing.

As an accompaniment to the tip line, the DEA has sent packets of educational materials to twelve hundred pharmacies in the Atlanta, Georgia, metropolitan area. The packet includes information about the tip line and a guide that points out suspicious signs that pharmacy employees should watch out for. These include written prescriptions with all words spelled out and in perfect handwriting (not the norm for doctors) and customers who return to the pharmacy often, among others. According to Harry S. Sommers, who is special agent in charge of the DEA's Atlanta Field Division, the texting program allows people to play a role in preventing painkiller abuse. "This method of communication," he says, "is a great opportunity for the public to anonymously engage in the fight against state-wide prescription drug abuse while keeping up with today's technology."[84]

More Federal Efforts

The US Department of Health and Human Services (HHS) has also taken steps to clamp down on opioid painkiller abuse in the United States. This has long been an issue of concern for the agency, as well as for its director, Sylvia M. Burwell, who calls it a "devastating epidemic facing our nation."[85] The HHS approach

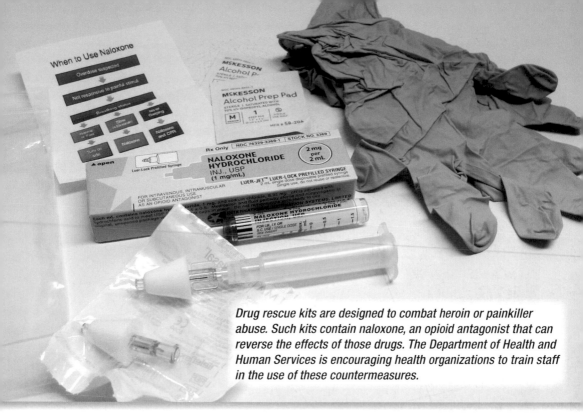

Drug rescue kits are designed to combat heroin or painkiller abuse. Such kits contain naloxone, an opioid antagonist that can reverse the effects of those drugs. The Department of Health and Human Services is encouraging health organizations to train staff in the use of these countermeasures.

features three priority areas that focus on prevention, treatment, and intervention.

First, it will provide financial resources to train and educate health care professionals. This is considered one of the most essential steps toward preventing opioid abuse and addiction. Second, the HHS will assume a lead role in expanding the use and distribution of naloxone, an opioid antagonist drug (sometimes called an anti-opioid drug) that can reverse the effects of opioids and potentially save the lives of overdose victims. Finally, the HHS will expand the use of medication-assisted treatment for opioid addicts. This will involve awarding millions of dollars in funding to states, which can use the money to enhance and expand their treatment programs for people with opioid use disorders.

The HHS will also work with legislators to create bipartisan laws that require training for safe opioid prescribing and establish new opioid prescribing guidelines for chronic pain. Says NIDA director Nora D. Volkow of the new initiative, "I am very excited to see the commitment and support at the highest levels of the HHS to address the opioid crisis in our country."[86]

A Teen Takes Action

Kaegan Casey knew that many of his high school friends were abusing opioid painkillers, and he was troubled by that. But when his friend Kelly Johnson died of an overdose, he knew he had to do something to save other kids from the same fate. So for his senior project, he created a documentary called *The Other Side of Andover, Massachusetts*, about his hometown. During the making of the film, Casey interviewed current and former Andover High School students, including one young man who had switched to heroin after becoming addicted to painkillers. Also featured was a young woman who was only fourteen the first time she saw someone shoot heroin. About twenty of her friends have tried it, and thirteen or fourteen of them use it regularly.

When the film was uploaded to YouTube, it received more than eleven thousand views within the first week. Casey was pleased at the positive feedback he received—and happy that there had been no backlash. People thanked him for creating it, saying that they had no idea of the seriousness of Andover's opioid problem. Parents began using the film as a conversation starter to discuss drugs with their kids. Andover police commander Charles Heseltine even praised Casey for highlighting the issue. "It's not just a police problem," says Heseltine. "It's a whole community problem. I think (Casey) has done a great job of making people aware."

Quoted in Tim Lima, "'Other Side of Andover;' Student's Documentary Brings Heroin Epidemic Home," *Andover Townsman*, June 9, 2015. http://m.andovertownsman.com.

State Actions

Another HHS agency, the CDC, has launched an initiative called Prescription Drug Overdose Prevention for States. Through this program, for which the CDC has allocated $20 million, states can receive funding that helps their health departments develop creative opioid abuse prevention efforts, as well as implement safer prescribing practices. In March 2015, when CDC officials announced the new program, states were invited to submit applications for funding. The states with the highest overdose rates in the United States were given the highest priority.

In September 2015 the CDC announced that sixteen states had been awarded from $750,000 to $1 million each in federal funds. The states were Arizona, California, Illinois, Kentucky, Nebraska, New Mexico, North Carolina, Ohio, Oklahoma, Oregon, Pennsylvania, Rhode Island, Tennessee, Utah, Vermont, and Wisconsin. "The prescription drug overdose epidemic is tragic and costly, but can be reversed,"[87] says CDC director Thomas Frieden. The CDC will continue awarding grants to states through 2019; according to Frieden, the ultimate goal is for all fifty states to implement prevention programs.

Whether they are recipients of such grants or not, many states have taken the initiative to address painkiller abuse and addiction. In Alabama, for instance, health officials launched the Zero Addiction Prescription Drug Abuse Prevention Campaign in June 2015. The program includes radio and television advertising that will spread awareness about the dangers of abusing painkillers and other prescription drugs. Another component of Alabama's program is a website called Zero Addiction. Visitors to the site can find addiction treatment information for their county, as well as provide anonymous tips to law enforcement on suspicious drug activity.

In Ohio—where 21 percent of high school students have abused painkillers—a law passed in December 2014 requires school districts to educate students about opioid abuse. In Massachusetts, state senators introduced a bill that would require all public school districts to screen seventh and tenth graders for opioid use. In Oregon, which has the country's second-highest rate of nonmedical use of prescription opioids, former governor (and former emergency medicine physician) John Kitzhaber appointed a special task force to address the problem. The group presented its initiative in late 2014, which includes five action steps: (1) reduce the number of painkiller pills in circulation; (2) educate prescribers and the public on the risks of opioid use; (3) foster safe disposal of unused medication; (4) provide treatment for opioid dependence; and (5) request continued leadership from the governor and health professionals.

Tyler's Light

As federal and state governments implement programs to help prevent painkiller abuse in the United States, private individuals are also getting involved. Many of these are people who have lost loved ones to opioid overdose; as a way of coping with their grief, they want to help prevent others from suffering. This was the case with Wayne and Christy Campbell from Pickerington, Ohio, whose twenty-one-year-old son, Tyler, died of an overdose. A talented three-sport athlete in high school, Tyler had surgery on his shoulder during his sophomore year of college. Afterward, doctors sent him home with a prescription for sixty Percocet. His parents were unaware that when the painkillers were gone, Tyler continued getting them from his teammates and friends. When they found out, they enrolled him in a rehab program, and then a second program when he relapsed. After completing the second treatment program, Tyler seemed better and even talked with his parents about wanting to be a drug counselor. Then on the morning of July 22, 2011, just twelve hours after her son returned home from rehab, Christy found him dead in his bedroom from a heroin overdose.

> "When you think you're the last family in the community that it could happen to, you'll be proved wrong."[89]
>
> —Wayne Campbell, whose son, Tyler, died from a drug overdose.

The Campbells were devastated over Tyler's death and vowed to do something to save other young people from the same fate. Within a few weeks they had founded an organization in his memory called Tyler's Light. "It's too late for Tyler," says Wayne, "but there are other Tylers out there."[88] Since they founded Tyler's Light, the Campbells have traveled to six states and given presentations to an estimated eighty thousand kids. One of the schools they visited in April 2015 was Indian Lake High School in Lewistown, Ohio. In a packed auditorium, before students, teachers, and parents, Wayne talked about Tyler and what happened to him as a result of opioid addiction. He told students that if they suspect a friend is using drugs, never hesitate to tell someone, because they could be saving a life. He also shared alarming drug-related statistics, such as the fact that more people in Ohio overdose each year on painkillers or heroin than are killed in automobile accidents.

Then, toward the end of his presentation, Wayne passed along a warning to parents: to educate themselves, be alert, and ask tough questions even if their kids do not like it. He reminded them that painkiller addiction and heroin addiction affect people from all walks of life, no matter their economic or social status. "When you think you're the last family in the community that it could happen to," Wayne said, "you'll be proved wrong."[89]

Focus on Young Athletes

Presentations like those given by the Campbells have proved to be extraordinarily effective in increasing awareness of the dangers of opioids. The problem is that such programs are rare; although drug abuse and addiction are age-old problems, the painkiller

Young athletes are vulnerable to painkiller abuse because they often receive injuries that require pain management. Although some counselors have taken up the cause of informing athletes of the risks, they are sometimes met with resistance from schools that are unwilling to acknowledge the problem.

abuse epidemic is relatively recent. Thus, established, tried-and-true prevention programs do not yet exist. "High schools don't have a lot of people coming in and speaking about prescription drugs,"[90] says drug and alcohol counselor Marcus Amos. For years Amos has worked to raise awareness about the prolific use of painkillers among student athletes. In 2005 he founded Prevention Education for Athletes, a program that addresses painkiller addiction as a result of sports injuries, as well as overdose deaths among athletes. Amos has run into numerous stumbling blocks along the way; through personal experience, he has learned that colleges do not want to talk about drug use among athletes. It is a subject that Amos has found to be taboo, yet he does not let that stop him. He is fully committed to educating kids about the dangers of opioid drugs.

> "High schools don't have a lot of people coming in and speaking about prescription drugs."[90]
>
> —Marcus Amos, a drug and alcohol counselor who created the Prevention Education for Athletes program.

Amos regularly speaks at schools and sports campuses about the prevalence and dangers of painkiller abuse. He is convinced that painkiller education programs are badly needed in schools throughout the United States. Teens, he has learned, have the perception that the drugs are not dangerous—and they have no hesitation about using them. "It's a reckless cultural behavior at this age," says Amos. He urges high school administrators to be proactive about painkiller and other drug awareness, rather than reactive. "You can't wait for kids to die,"[91] he says. Amos's hope is that as awareness about the painkiller problem continues to grow, this will compel individuals and groups to develop education and awareness programs aimed at young people.

NOPE

The Narcotics Overdose Prevention and Education, or NOPE for short, is one of those programs. It was founded in 2004 in Palm Beach County, Florida, by a group of parents who have lost children to drug-related incidents, along with other members of the community. The NOPE program is designed to educate middle

Veterans in Pain

As a way to tackle the widespread abuse of painkillers in the United States, government officials have taken steps to make the drugs harder to get. During the summer of 2014, for instance, the DEA enacted a measure that vastly restricted the availability of hydrocodone combination drugs such as Vicodin. Although the move was hailed by drug addiction experts and pain management specialists, one group is suffering because of it: US military veterans who suffer from chronic pain. According to the VA, more than half a million veterans take prescription opioid painkillers.

One of them is Craig Schroeder, who was severely injured during a bomb explosion while serving in Iraq. Schroeder suffers from traumatic brain injury, as well as pain related to a broken foot and ankle and a herniated disc in his back. He has regularly taken painkillers since leaving the military; once the DEA restrictions were in place, however, his doctor was no longer allowed to call in a prescription. Thus, Schroeder was forced to wait months for a doctor's appointment, and for much of that time he was confined to bed. "It was a nightmare," he says. "I was just in unbearable, terrible pain. I couldn't even go to the ER because those doctors won't write those [prescriptions]." The VA has been accused of grossly overprescribing painkillers to military veterans, and advocates of the new regulation say it could help curtail that practice. Still, people like Schroeder who depend on opioids for chronic pain feel like their needs are being cast aside.

Quoted in Emily Wax-Thibodeaux, "New Rules on Narcotic Painkillers Cause Grief for Veterans and VA," *Washington Post*, February 18, 2015. www.washingtonpost.com.

school and high school students about the dangers of abusing prescription painkillers. This program differs from the general drug education programs of the past because it specifically addresses painkiller abuse among teens. Since NOPE's founding, it has grown substantially. As a March 2015 article by the Lighthouse Recovery Institute explains: "What started as a group of concerned citizens presenting information in local schools has grown into a national organization that targets all areas of painkiller abuse, from education to advocacy and beyond."[92]

NOPE is also different from older drug programs because it does not use scare tactics; such efforts have proved to be ineffective with young people. Instead, NOPE presentations show students the facts—the brutally honest, often shocking reality of opioid abuse and addiction. During one presentation, for instance, students in Pennsylvania sat in stunned silence after hearing the 911 tape of a mother finding her seventeen-year-old son dead from a painkiller overdose. Another important element of the program is a dynamic multimedia presentation, which teaches students about the science of addiction. The NOPE organization says this presentation is "purposefully blunt and evokes powerful emotions."[93] There are also guest speakers who have lost loved ones to painkiller overdose. These people talk frankly about their grief and their dedication to help save other young people from the same fate.

On January 30, 2014, a NOPE presentation was held at a high school in Delaware County, Pennsylvania. One of the speakers was Tricia Stouch, who talked to the students about her nineteen-year-old daughter, Pamela. For a number of years the young woman had battled addiction, starting with Percocet, then OxyContin, and then heroin. She went through rehab several times but could not stay clean or beat her addiction. On March 27, 2010, after a long, painful battle, Pamela died of a heroin overdose. "It's too late for my daughter," Tricia told the students. "But I might be able to help somebody else's child."[94]

> "It's too late for my daughter. But I might be able to help somebody else's child."[94]
>
> —Tricia Stouch, whose daughter, Pamela, was addicted to painkillers and heroin and died from an overdose.

Later in 2014 parents in East Marlborough, Pennsylvania, attended a NOPE presentation at Unionville High School. The presenters shared alarming statistics about painkillers, such as Pennsylvania being the seventh-highest state for drug overdoses in the United States. Parents watched a powerful film that showed picture after picture of teens who had died of a drug overdose. One of the presenters was Jacquelene Zwaan, who shared her personal story about losing her son R.J. to a painkiller overdose in 2008. She described him as a model son, her very best friend, someone she thought talked to her about anything—but he "never talked about that," she says. Zwaan had no idea that her son was taking pills, and that is why she now speaks in public about her heartbreaking loss. "I died the day that RJ did,"[95] she says. She hopes that by sharing her story with other parents, she can help them avoid the unbearable pain of losing a child.

Hope and Uncertainty

Painkiller abuse and addiction is a formidable problem in the United States—one that will not be easy to solve. This is largely because the American public is still not aware of how serious the problem is, or even that the problem exists. The creators of programs such as Tyler's Light, NOPE, and Prevention Education for Athletes are working to change that. Initiatives on the part of the federal government and individual states are also making inroads in addressing the problem. In time, it is hoped that such initiatives will raise awareness, offer people treatment, and above all, save lives.

SOURCE NOTES

Chapter 1: How Serious a Problem Is Painkiller Abuse?

1. Quoted in Bob Segal, "The Enemy at Home: Veterans Addicted and Dying from VA Pain Pills," WTHR, April 25, 2014. www.wthr.com.
2. Quoted in Segal, "The Enemy at Home."
3. Quoted in Jim Axelrod, "VA's Overmedication of Vets Widespread, Inspector General Finds," CBS News, May 14, 2014. www.cbsnews.com.
4. Quoted in Chris Iliades, "When Veterans Cope with Chronic Pain," Everyday Health, December 6, 2013. www.everyday health.com.
5. Robert N. Jamison and Jianren Mao, "Opioid Analgesics," Mayo Clinic Proceedings, July 2015. www.mayoclinicpro ceedings.org.
6. Quoted in Karen Cicero, "The 10 Most Painful Conditions," Prevention, December 12, 2014. www.prevention.com.
7. Quoted in Elizabeth Landau, "From a Tree, a 'Miracle' Called Aspirin," CNN, December 22, 2010. www.cnn.com.
8. Francis Collins, "Managing Chronic Pain: Opioids Are Often Not the Answer," NIH Director's Blog, National Institutes of Health, January 27, 2015. http://directorsblog.nih.gov.
9. Leslie Kendall Dye, "But What If I Actually Need Painkillers?," Salon, July 26, 2015. www.salon.com.
10. Quoted in Harvard Health Letter, "Caution: These Are the Most Addictive Pain Meds," November 1, 2013. www.health .harvard.edu.
11. Mayo Clinic, "Prescription Drug Abuse," December 5, 2014. www.mayoclinic.org.
12. Nora D. Volkow, "From the Director," National Institute on Drug Abuse, November 2014. www.drugabuse.gov.

13. Quoted in Alan Mozes, "Who's at Risk for Narcotic Painkiller Addiction?," WebMD, July 7, 2015. www.webmd.com.
14. Hazelden Betty Ford Institute for Recovery Advocacy, "Response to the Opioid Crisis," white paper, 2015. www.hazeldenbettyford.org.
15. Quoted in Sara G. Miller, "OxyContin Approved for Kids, Worrying Doctors," LiveScience, October 6, 2015. www.livescience.com.
16. Quoted in Catherine Saint Louis, "F.D.A. Approval of OxyContin Use for Children Continues to Draw Scrutiny," *New York Times*, October 8, 2015. www.nytimes.com.
17. Joanna Shepherd, "Combating the Prescription Painkiller Epidemic: A National Prescription Drug Reporting Program," *American Journal of Law & Medicine*, March 2014. http://jlm.sagepub.com.
18. Quoted in Brian Krans, "Report: Many High-Risk Opioid Users Get Pills by Prescription," Healthline, www.healthline.com.
19. Quoted in WUSA, "Teenagers Getting Prescription Drugs Online," June 10, 2013. www.wusa9.com.
20. Nora D. Volkow, "What Is the Federal Government Doing to Combat the Opioid Abuse Epidemic?," testimony before congressional subcommittee, National Institute on Drug Abuse, May 1, 2015. www.drugabuse.gov.
21. Collins, "Managing Chronic Pain."

Chapter 2: What Are the Effects of Painkillers?

22. Quoted in Thomas H. Maugh II, "Scientist Discovered Opiate Receptor," *Los Angeles Times*, September 24, 2013. http://articles.latimes.com.
23. National Alliance of Advocates for Buprenorphine Treatment, "How Do Opioids Work in the Brain?," December 2008. www.naabt.org.
24. National Alliance of Advocates for Buprenorphine Treatment, "How Do Opioids Work in the Brain?"

25. Quoted in Marvin D. Seppala, "Opioids and How They Work," excerpt from *Prescription Painkillers*. Center City, MN: Hazelden, 2010. www.hazelden.org.

26. Quoted in Sarah T. Williams, "What's It Really like to Withdraw from Heroin and Painkillers?," *Minneapolis (MN) Post*, February 14, 2014. www.minnpost.com.

27. Jeffrey F. Scherrer et al., "Prescription Opioid Analgesics Increase the Risk of Depression," *Journal of General Internal Medicine*, March 2014. www.ncbi.nlm.nih.gov.

28. Quoted in Cleveland Clinic Family Health Team, "The Down Side and Side Effects of Painkillers," July 1, 2013. http://health.clevelandclinic.org.

29. International Foundation for Functional Gastrointestinal Disorders, "Narcotic Bowel Syndrome," August 22, 2013. www.iffgd.org.

30. Quoted in Group Health Research Institute, "Opioids Linked to Higher Risk of Pneumonia in Older Adults," September 22, 2011. www.grouphealthresearch.org.

31. Quoted in Shelly Burgess, "FDA Limits Acetaminophen in Prescription Combination Products; Requires Liver Toxicity Warnings," news release, Food and Drug Administration, January 13, 2011. www.fda.gov.

32. Nora D. Volkow, "What Science Tells Us About Opioid Abuse and Addiction," testimony before the House Committee on Energy and Commerce Subcommittee on Oversight and Investigations, May 1, 2015. https://olpa.od.nih.gov.

33. Quoted in American Society of Anesthesiologists, "More than 14 Percent of Pregnant Women Prescribed Opioids," *Newswise*, February 12, 2014. www.newswise.com.

34. Quoted in Elaine Quijano, "Life Begins with Agony of Withdrawal for Opiate-Addicted Babies," CBS News, July 8, 2015. www.cbsnews.com.

35. Seppala, "Opioids and How They Work."

36. Seppala, "Opioids and How They Work."

37. Quoted in Peter Jaret, "When Pain Kills," AARP, September 2015. www.aarp.org.

38. Volkow, "What Science Tells Us About Opioid Abuse and Addiction."

39. Maia Szalavitz, "How Not to Die like Heath Ledger, Part II," *Huffington Post*, February 6, 2008. www.huffingtonpost.com.
40. Sanjay Gupta, "The Truth About Prescription Medication Addiction," *The Chart* (blog), CNN, February 22, 2012. http://the chart.blogs.cnn.com.

Chapter 3: How Addictive Are Painkillers?

41. Elizabeth Foy Larsen, "Good Teens Turned Drug Addicts," *Huffington Post*, September 24, 2014. www.huffingtonpost .com.
42. National Institute on Drug Abuse, "DrugFacts: Understanding Drug Abuse and Addiction," November 2012. www.drug abuse.gov.
43. Harvard Medical School, "Understanding Addiction," Help-Guide.org. www.helpguide.org.
44. Harvard Medical School, "Understanding Addiction."
45. Charles P. O'Brien, "Physical Dependence and Addiction," National Alliance of Advocates for Buprenorphine Treatment," 2014. www.naabt.org.
46. Quoted in Alvin Powell, "Heroin's Descent," *Harvard Gazette*, September 29, 2015. http://news.harvard.edu.
47. Nicholas Kardaras, "The 'Accidental Addict': Soccer Moms, Painkillers and Addiction," Fox News, June 20, 2014. www .foxnews.com.
48. Quoted in Larsen, "Good Teens Turned Drug Addicts."
49. Quoted in National Safety Council, "Nearly Half of Opioid Painkiller Users Unaware They Are Taking Drugs as Addictive as Heroin," news release, June 23, 2015. www.nsc.org.
50. Lindsay Kramer, "Why Is Opiate Addiction So Hard to Treat?," Recovery.org Pro Corner, February 25, 2015. www.recovery .org.
51. Seppala, "Opioids and How They Work."
52. Quoted in Williams, "What's It Really like to Withdraw from Heroin and Painkillers?"
53. Quoted in Robin Young and Jeremy Hobson, "Doctor: Prescription Painkillers Kill More People than Heroin," *Here & Now*, WBUR, September 9, 2015. https://hereandnow.wbur .org.

54. Quoted in Young and Hobson, "Doctor."
55. Quoted in Peter Eisler, "Older Americans Hooked on Rx: 'I Was a Zombie,'" *USA Today*, May 22, 2014. www.usatoday.com.
56. Quoted in Eisler, "Older Americans Hooked on Rx."
57. Quoted in Benedict Carey, "Prescription Painkillers Seen as a Gateway to Heroin," *New York Times*, February 10, 2014. www.nytimes.com.
58. Quoted in Susan Svrluga, "Fairfax Mother of Young Heroin Addict: 'There Were Clues. But We Had No Clue,'" *Washington Post*, April 22, 2014. www.washingtonpost.com.
59. Quoted in L. Jon Wertheim and Ken Rodriguez, "How Painkillers Are Turning Young Athletes into Heroin Addicts," *Sports Illustrated*, June 18, 2015. www.si.com.

Chapter 4: Treatment and Recovery Challenges

60. Celine Gounder, "Who Is Responsible for the Pain-Pill Epidemic?," *New Yorker*, November 8, 2013. www.newyorker.com.
61. Quoted in Kimberly Leonard, "Breaking Heroin's Hold," *U.S. News & World Report*, July 10, 2015. www.usnews.com.
62. Gounder, "Who Is Responsible for the Pain-Pill Epidemic?"
63. Gounder, "Who Is Responsible for the Pain-Pill Epidemic?"
64. Quoted in Andy Steiner, "Chronic Pain Sufferers Find Prescription Painkillers Ineffective for Long-Term Relief, Survey Reports," *MinnPost*, October 31, 2014. www.minnpost.com.
65. Quoted in Steiner, "Chronic Pain Sufferers Find Prescription Painkillers Ineffective for Long-Term Relief, Survey Reports."
66. Peter Przekop, *Chronic Pain in America: Consequences, Addiction and Treatment*. Rancho Mirage, CA: Betty Ford Center, 2014. http://docplayer.net.
67. Quoted in Przekop, *Chronic Pain in America*.
68. Quoted in Rebecca Hiscott, "Rethink Chronic Pain," *Neurology Now*, August/September 2015. https://patients.aan.com.
69. Quoted in Hiscott, "Rethink Chronic Pain."
70. Quoted in James McIntosh, "Acupuncture Back Pain Success Determined by Psychological Factors," Medical News Today, February 16, 2015. www.medicalnewstoday.com.

71. Quoted in McIntosh, "Acupuncture Back Pain Success Determined by Psychological Factors."
72. National Institutes of Health, "Cognitive Behavioral Therapy for Back Pain," MedlinePlus, October 14, 2013. www.nlm.nih.gov.
73. Quoted in Abdul-Kareem Ahmed, "Cognitive Behavioral Therapy Changes Gray Matter Morphology in Chronic Pain," Pain Research Forum, November 25, 2013. www.painresearchforum.org.
74. Austin Frakt, "Dealing with Opioid Abuse Would Pay for Itself," *New York Times*, August 4, 2014. www.nytimes.com.
75. Charles H. Silberstein, "Essay: A Counter to Addiction," *MV Times*, January 2, 2014. www.mvtimes.com.
76. Silberstein, "Essay."
77. NYU Langone Medical Center, "Opioid Relapse Rates Fall After Jail Release, According to Pilot Study," April 14, 2015. http://nyulangone.org.
78. Quoted in Iliades, "When Veterans Cope with Chronic Pain."

Chapter 5: How Can Painkiller Abuse Be Prevented?

79. Quoted in Claudia Lauer and Alicia A. Caldwell, "DEA Raids Clinics, Pharmacies, in 'Pill Mill' Crackdown," *Washington Times*, May 20, 2015. www.washingtontimes.com.
80. Quoted in Mark Potter, "Drug Enforcement Administration Raids 'Pill Mills' in Four Southern States," NBC News, May 20, 2015. www.nbcnews.com.
81. Quoted in Drug Enforcement Administration, "DEA to Publish Final Rule Rescheduling Hydrocodone Combination Products," August 21, 2014. www.dea.gov.
82. Quoted in Emily Wax-Thibodeaux, "New Rules on Narcotic Painkillers Cause Grief for Veterans and VA," *Washington Post*, February 18, 2015. www.washingtonpost.com.
83. Quoted in Jen Christensen, "DEA Turns to Texting to Fight Prescription Drug Abuse," CNN.com, February 21, 2014. www.cnn.com.

84. Quoted in Drug Enforcement Administration, "DEA Atlanta Division Unveils Statewide Prescription Drug Texting Tip Line," February 20, 2014. www.dea.gov.
85. Quoted in US Department of Health and Human Services, "HHS Takes Strong Steps to Address Opioid-Drug Related Overdose, Death, and Dependence," news release, March 26, 2015. www.hhs.gov.
86. Nora D. Volkow, "HHS Announces Actions to Attack the Opioid Crisis," *Nora's Blog*, National Institute on Drug Abuse, March 26, 2015. www.drugabuse.gov.
87. Quoted in Centers for Disease Control and Prevention, "CDC Funding Helps States Combat Prescription Drug Overdose Epidemic," news release, September 4, 2015. www.cdc.gov.
88. Quoted in Kristine Meldrum Denholm, "In Depth: Perils of Painkillers for Young Athletes," *USA Today*, September 2, 2015. http://usatodayhss.com.
89. Quoted in Indian Lake High School, "Tyler's Light Assembly," April 28, 2015. http://hs.ils-k12.org.
90. Quoted in Denholm, "In Depth."
91. Quoted in Denholm, "In Depth."
92. Lighthouse Recovery Institute, "A New Take on Preventing Teenage Painkiller Abuse," March 4, 2015. http://light houserecoveryinstitute.com.
93. Narcotics Overdose Prevention and Education Task Force, "Middle and High School Presentations." www.nopetask force.org.
94. Quoted in Rose Quinn, "Delco Experts, Families Talk About Heroin Horrors," *Delaware County Daily Times* (Upper Darby Township, PA), February 8, 2015. www.nopetaskforce.org.
95. Quoted in Karen Cresta, "Parents Say Yep to Nope and Get Lifesaving Homework," *Unionville (PA) Times*, October 16, 2014. www.unionvilletimes.com.

ORGANIZATIONS TO CONTACT

American Society of Addiction Medicine (ASAM)

4601 N. Park Ave.
Upper Arcade, Suite 101
Chevy Chase, MD 20815-4520
phone: (301) 656-3920 • fax: (301) 656-3815
e-mail: e-mail@asam.org • website: www.asam.org

ASAM seeks to improve the quality of (and increase access to) addiction treatment, increase awareness of addiction, and support research and prevention efforts. Its website offers numerous articles, fact sheets, and other publications about painkiller addiction.

Centers for Disease Control and Prevention (CDC)

1600 Clifton Rd.
Atlanta, GA 30329-4027
phone: (800) 232-4636
website: www.cdc.gov

The United States' leading health protection agency, the CDC seeks to promote health and quality of life by controlling disease, injury, and disability. Its website features numerous articles, fact sheets, and policy statements about prescription drug abuse, including painkillers.

Drug Enforcement Administration (DEA)

2401 Jefferson Davis Hwy.
Alexandria, VA 22301
phone: (202) 307-1000; toll-free: (800) 332-4288
website: www.dea.gov

The DEA is the United States' top federal drug law enforcement agency. Its website links to a separate site called Just Think Twice (www.justthinktwice.com) that is designed for teenagers and features fact sheets, personal experiences, and numerous publications about painkillers and other drugs of abuse.

Drug Free America Foundation

5999 Central Ave., Suite 301
St. Petersburg, FL 33710
phone: (727) 828-0211 • fax: (727) 828-0212
e-mail: webmaster@dfaf.org • website: www.dfaf.org

The Drug Free America Foundation is a drug prevention and policy organization. Its website has a search engine that produces numerous articles about painkillers and other prescription drugs, as well as links to a teen-focused site called Students Taking Action Not Drugs, or STAND.

Foundation for a Drug-Free World

1626 N. Wilcox Ave., Suite 1297
Los Angeles, CA 90028
phone: (818) 952-5260; toll-free: (888) 668-6378
e-mail: info@drugfreeworld.org • website: www.drugfreeworld.org

The Foundation for a Drug-Free World exists to empower young people with facts about drugs so they can make good decisions and live drug free. A wealth of information about painkillers and other prescription drugs is available on its website, including videos, fact sheets, and personal stories of teens who have fought addiction.

National Council on Alcoholism and Drug Dependence (NCADD)

217 Broadway, Suite 712
New York, NY 10007
phone: (212) 269-7797 • fax: (212) 269-7510
e-mail: national@ncadd.org • website: http://ncadd.org

The NCADD is a leading advocacy organization whose focus is addressing alcoholism and drug dependence. Its website offers numerous articles and stories about drug abuse (including painkillers) and addiction, as well as a link to the NCADD blog.

National Institute on Drug Abuse (NIDA)

National Institutes of Health
6001 Executive Blvd., Room 5213
Bethesda, MD 20892-9561
phone: (301) 443-1124
e-mail: information@nida.nih.gov • website: www.drugabuse.gov

NIDA supports research efforts and ensures the rapid dissemination of research to improve drug abuse prevention, treatment, and policy. The website links to a separate NIDA for Teens site, which is designed especially for teenagers and provides a wealth of information about illicit drug use (including the abuse of painkillers) and addiction.

Office of National Drug Control Policy

750 Seventeenth St. NW
Washington, DC 20503
phone: (800) 666-3332 • fax: (202) 395-6708
e-mail: ondcp@ncjrs.org • website: www.whitehouse.gov/ondcp

A component of the Executive Office of the President, the Office of National Drug Control Policy is responsible for directing the federal government's antidrug programs. A wealth of information about painkillers can be produced through the website's search engine.

Partnership for Drug-Free Kids

352 Park Ave. S., 9th Floor
New York, NY 10010
phone: (212) 922-1560 • fax: (212) 922-1570
website: www.drugfree.org

Partnership for Drug-Free Kids is dedicated to helping parents and families solve the teenage substance abuse problem. Its website offers numerous publications about painkiller abuse, as well as a video about teen prescription drug abuse called *Out of Reach*, which was created by a teen filmmaker.

Substance Abuse and Mental Health Services Administration (SAMHSA)

1 Choke Cherry Rd.
Rockville, MD 20857
phone: (877) 726-4727 • fax: (240) 221-4292
e-mail: samhsainfo@samhsa.hhs.gov
website: www.samhsa.gov

SAMHSA's mission is to reduce the impact of substance abuse and mental illness on America's communities. The site offers a wealth of information about substance abuse, and numerous publications related to painkillers are available through its search engine.

FOR FURTHER RESEARCH

Books

Taite Adams, *Opiate Addiction*. St. Petersburg, FL: Rapid Response, 2015.

Beth Darnall, *Less Pain, Fewer Pills*. Boulder, CO: Bull, 2014.

Mark James Estren, *Prescription Drug Abuse*. Berkeley, CA: Ronin, 2013.

Joani Gammill, *Painkillers, Heroin, and the Road to Sanity*. Center City, MN: Hazelden, 2014.

Sam Quinones, *Dreamland: The True Tale of America's Opiate Epidemic*. New York: Bloomsbury, 2015.

Rosa Waters, *Prescription Painkillers*. Broomall, PA: Mason Crest, 2015.

Internet Sources

Abby Haglage, "Painkiller Overdoses Kill More than One American Every Hour," Daily Beast, July 1, 2014. www.thedailybeast.com/articles/2014/07/01/america-s-prescription-opiate-problem-isn-t-going-anywhere.html.

Elizabeth Foy Larsen, "Good Teens Turned Drug Addicts," *Huffington Post*, September 24, 2014. www.huffingtonpost.com/2014/09/24/teens-turned-drug-addicts_n_5877306.html.

Kimberly Leonard, "Teens with Addiction Have Few Recovery Programs," *U.S. News & World Report*, June 10, 2014. http://health.usnews.com/health-news/best-childrens-hospitals/articles/2014/06/10/teens-with-addiction-have-few-recovery-programs.

A. Pawlowski, "Secret Life of Teens: The Dangerous Drug Parents Aren't Talking About with Kids," *Today*, September 19, 2014.

www.today.com/parents/prescription-drug-abuse-part-secret -life-teens-1D80157066.

L. Jon Wertheim and Ken Rodriguez, "How Painkillers Are Turning Young Athletes into Heroin Addicts," *Sports Illustrated*, June 18, 2015. www.si.com/more-sports/2015/06/18/special-report -painkillers-young-athletes-heroin-addicts.

Robin Young and Jeremy Hobson, "Doctor: Prescription Painkillers Kill More People than Heroin," *Here & Now*, WBUR, September 9, 2015. https://hereandnow.wbur.org/2015/09/09/heroin -epidemic-overprescribing.

Saundra Young, "Medical Marijuana Laws May Reduce Painkiller Overdoses," CNN, August 26, 2014. www.cnn.com/2014/08/25 /health/medical-marijuana-overdose-deaths.

Websites

Medicine Abuse Project (http://medicineabuseproject.org). The Medicine Abuse Project is a five-year action campaign with an aggressive goal of preventing half a million teens from abusing medicine by the year 2017. Its website offers information about prevention of prescription drug abuse, painkiller addiction, and over-the-counter medicine abuse, as well as stories, news articles, and a drug guide.

Mothers Against Prescription Drug Abuse (http://mapdaonline. org). This advocacy group was created to increase public awareness about the dangers of prescription drug abuse and addiction, while dispelling the myth that the drugs are safe. The website offers a wealth of information for parents, teens, and educators.

National Coalition Against Prescription Drug Abuse (http:// ncapda.org) Founded in memory of twenty-one-year-old Joey Rovero, who died of a prescription drug overdose, NCAPDA partners with schools, community organizations, and other agencies to increase awareness about prescription drug abuse/ misuse. The website offers personal stories, news release, videos, and numerous publications about painkiller abuse and addiction.

INDEX

Note: Boldface page numbers indicate illustrations.

PICTURE CREDITS